# Back - 2 - Back

• TOURISM

Hanol Publishing

STUDENT'S BOOK 1

# Introduction

Back-2-Back Tourism is the second book in the series that focuses on communicative skills rather than grammar. This course is tailored for high beginners to low intermediate students seeking a career in the tourism industry. Its primary aim is to provide the students with the necessary skills to effectively communicate with the general public in everyday situations. Back-2-Back Tourism is an activity based textbook that makes learning enjoyable. Each chapter is divided into the following sections:

## KEY VOCABULARY

The key vocabulary section focuses on tourism related vocabulary. This vocabulary will be used, reinforced and recycled throughout the chapter. In this approach students will have ample opportunities to use the vocabulary in various situations.

## WARM-UP

The warm-up section starts with a simple exercise that reinforces the vocabulary. In this section the students get more familiar and comfortable using the words. A variety of exercises are used to reinforce this.

## LANGUAGE STRUCTURE

This section introduces many expressions required in the tourism industry. The exercises help students use the language more effectively.

## CONVERSATION

Every conversation presents a realistic situation that the students may encounter. It is divided into a main dialogue and a substitution drill. First, the students practice the dialogue with a partner until they have mastered it. After that, the students get to practice new expressions and vocabulary. Finally, the class brainstorms possible solutions to deal with the situation at hand.

## CHALLENGE YOURSELF

This section is structured to challenge students. The activities will make students think further about the topic. Students will use many of the expressions and vocabulary that they have learned in the chapter to complete a task.

## PAIR WORK

Pair Work provides an opportunity for students to practice the language that they have studied. It is designed to maximize the students talking time. Students interact with each other and share information in order to complete the task. In this section, students have a chance to role play different situations that they may encounter in their jobs. Genuine communication takes place during this exercise.

## READING

We have chosen a variety of interesting tourism related topics. All the readings will give the students a more rounded knowledge of the tourism industry. Comprehension exercises are included to develop reading skills that they will use throughout their career.

## ONE MORE TIME

This section makes Back-2-Back a unique and enjoyable textbook. All of the language games provide students with another opportunity to speak in a more relaxed and fun atmosphere. These structured activities will motivate and encourage the students to freely use the language that they have studied.

## Authors' Acknowledgments

There are so many people that made our vision of producing Back-2-Back Tourism possible. First and foremost we would like to thank the Tourism students at Jangan College. Our students inspired us and gave us some ideas on what to include. They helped us to pilot the project and provided invaluable feedback on many of the activities. To them we say: "Thank-You".

We are grateful to everyone at Hanol Publishing for their tireless efforts and their willingness to produce a "different" kind of textbook, is appreciated.

Special appreciation goes to Lee Min-Young and Kim Seung Yeon of Singapore Airlines who were willing to have their photograph on the front cover; Objectif Travel in Morocco; Petra Haid from Lufthansa Airlines; the staff at Rick's Café in Casablanca, Morocco; Oberoi Mena House in Cairo, Egypt; Ritz Carlton Hotel, Sharm El Sheikh, Egypt and Mala Mala Game Reserve, South Africa.

We also like to thank the manager and staff at Jnan Palace Hotel in Fes, Morocco who graciously allowed us to photograph their staff. We are grateful to Kamal at Riad Kniza in Marrakech, Morocco who provided authentic material and put his staff at our disposal.

We would like to thank the following for the use of their logos and pictures; Club Med; Shangri-la Hotels and Resorts; Caesar palace Hotel; Excalibur Hotel; Burj Al Aerab Hotel; the Ice Hotel in Jukkasjarvi, Sweden; Jules'Undersea Lodge in Key Largo, Florida; Hilton Maldives Resorts and Spa; Oakwood; Mandarin Oriental Hotel Group, Raffles Hotel Group, Marriot Hotels and Resorts; Swisshotels and Resorts; The Peninsula Manila; Le Royal Meridian Bristol in Warsaw, Poland; Westin Hotel and Resorts and Gramercy Tavern Restaurant in New York City. We would also like to thank the following airlines: Emirates Airline, Cathay Pacific Airline, United Airline, Cebu Pacific Airline, Northwest Airline, British Airways; Air Canada; Thai International: Aero Mexico; Air China; Delta Airlines; Austrian Airlines; Gulf Air; Air Jamaica; Avianca; Alitalia; South African Airlines; and Olympic Airlines. Special thanks go to Indonesia Board of Tourism and Jordan Tourist Board.

Last but not least we are grateful to all our friends and colleagues who understood when we said, "We are writing". Especially Hee Jung Yoon who provided support, valuable insight, feedback on some of the activities in Back-2-Back Tourism, and her willingness to work with the publisher on our behalf.

All efforts were made to acknowledge everyone. Please contact the publisher for any omissions.

# CONTENTS

# Chapter 1

## *I'd Like To Change My Reservation, please.*

## ❶ KEY VOCABULARY

| | | | |
|---|---|---|---|
| Cellular Phone | Hold the line | Speaking | Cancel |
| Leave a message | Long Distance | Change | Memo |
| Wrong Number | Connect | Urgent | Unavailable |
| Busy | Transfer | Collect Call | A.S.A.P |
| Extension | Step Out | Local Call | Appointment |
| Call Back | Received | Requests | Meeting |

## ❷ WARM-UP

**A**

*MEMO*

ClubMed

To: Ms. Angie Pines Date: 08/10

*While You Were Out*

M: Mr. Jason Chang
OF: Pacific Travel
PHONE: (416) 225-2960

☐ Telephoned ☑ Please call
☐ Will call again ☑ Important **(1)**

**MESSAGE**: Wants to switch **(2)** the reservation from Aug.12th to 15th. Call him back right away **(3)**. Asks **(4)** for a copy of confirmation to be faxed.

Message taken **(5)** by: *Anna Goodman*

**B**

***Someone Called While You Were Out***

To: Mr. Jason Chang Date: Aug. 10th
From: Ms. Angie Pines Time: 3:45 pm
Of: Club Med Phone: (613) 828-1545

☐ Will call again ☐ Please call
☑ Returned your call

**MESSAGE:**

Your reservation has been switched to August 15th. The Deluxe room is unavailable, but we upgraded you to a Junior suite for the same price. Please inform my secretary of your fax number so we can fax you a copy of your new booking.

By: *Lucy Wong*

◆ **Look at Memo A. Substitute the shaded words with the words in the Key Vocabulary Box .**

**(1)** Important ➲ ________________
**(2)** Switch ➲ ________________
**(3)** Right away ➲ ________________
**(4)** Asks ➲ ________________
**(5)** Taken ➲ ________________

◆ **Look at Memo B. Answer the following questions in complete sentences.**

1. Who did Ms. Pines talk to?
2. Who was the message for?
3. Where does Ms. Pines work?
4. What did Ms. Pines want to receive from Mr. Chang?
5. What are the 2 changes made in the reservation?

## ❸ LANGUAGE STRUCTURE

| RECEPTIONIST | CALLER |
|---|---|
| Royal Palace Hotel. What can I do for you? | Yes, I'd like to change my reservation. |
| May I ask who's calling? | This is Mrs. McNeil from Rajah Travel. |
| Do you know the person who made your reservation? | His name is Mr. Willis. |
| He's busy right now. Would you like to leave a message? | Please have him call me back a.s.a.p. |
| Where can you be reached at? | I can be reached at 1-905-245-6700 ext. 302. |
| When is the best time for him to return your call? | Have him call me before 6 pm. |

| Mixed-up Sentences | | Rewrite the Sentences |
|---|---|---|
| contact / What's / your / Cook / number / Mr. | ➲ | ____________________? |
| back / do / expect / When / you / her | ➲ | ____________________? |
| the / give / I'll / message / Okay, / her / to | ➲ | ____________________. |
| to / like / to / Yes, / Ms. / I'd / speak / Roberts | ➲ | ____________________. |
| Travel. / Horizon / Blue / you / May / help / I | ➲ | ____________________? |
| telephone / have / Please / Cook / her / Mr. | ➲ | ____________________. |
| just / afraid / stepped / she / I'm / out | ➲ | ____________________. |
| ext.305 / reached / can / at / I / 617-285-6000/ be | ➲ | ____________________. |

◆ **Put the above sentences into a dialogue.**

**DIALOGUE**

**Receptionist:** ____________________

**Mr. Cook:** ____________________

**Receptionist:** ____________________

**Mr. Cook:** ____________________

**Receptionist:** ____________________

**Mr. Cook:** ____________________

**Receptionist:** ____________________

**Mr. Cook:** ____________________

◆ **Now practice the above dialogue with a partner.**

## ❹ CONVERSATION

➤ **Practice the following dialogue with a partner.**

**Receptionist:** Fantasy Island. **Please hold**... How may I direct your call? ①
**Caller:** **Mrs. Bryan**, please? ❶
**Receptionist:** I'll **transfer you**. I'm afraid the line is busy. Would you like to hold? ②
**Caller:** Yes, I'll hold.
**Receptionist:** Sorry to keep you waiting. Mrs. Bryan is **at a meeting**. ③
Do you want to leave a message?
**Caller:** No. I've already left **so many** messages. I want to speak to her right away. ❷
**Receptionist:** It's impossible. But I'll ask her to return your call **a.s.a.p**. ④
**Caller:** That's not good enough. I've been waiting for her call for **a week** now? ❸
**Receptionist:** I understand, sir. But she's not at her desk. I can only take a message.
**Caller:** I don't believe this! She's always **unavailable** every time I call. ❹
I must speak to her at once.

## SUBSTITUTION DRILL

➤ **Substitute with the words or phrases below:**

| Receptionist | Caller |
|---|---|
| ① Hold the line, please<br>Please wait a moment<br>Just a minute, please | ❶ May I talk to Mrs. Bryan,<br>I'd I like to speak to Mrs. Bryan<br>Mrs. Bryan's office |
| ② connect you<br>put you through<br>forward your call | ❷ lots<br>numerous<br>plenty of |
| ③ at a conference<br>at lunch<br>with a client | ❸ a few days<br>8 days<br>2 weeks |
| ④ right away<br>at once<br>immediately | ❹ busy<br>away from her desk<br>engaged / occupied |

## 5 CHALLENGE YOURSELF

◆ **Read the telephone conversation and answer the questions.**

Caller: __________ Contact No. __________

Company: ______________________________

Wanted to speak to: ____________________

Reasons for the call:

______________________________________

Who answered the call:

______________________________________

**DIALOGUE**

**Secretary:** Good Afternoon. Ramada Hotel. **Anna** speaking. How may I help you?

**Mr. Chang:** I'd like to speak to **Mr. Johnson**, please.

**Secretary:** I'm afraid he's **on the other line**. Do you want to leave a message?

**Mr. Chang:** Yes. Please have **him** call me back.

**Secretary:** Certainly. Could I have your name and contact number, please?

**Mr. Chang:** This is **Jason Chang** from **Pacific Travel**. I can be reached at **416-225-2960**.

**Secretary:** What are you calling in reference to?

**Mr. Chang:** I'd like **to book a conference room for 12 people on the 15th of August**.

**Secretary:** Thank-you, **Mr. Chang**. I'll forward your message to **him** right away. Have a pleasant day!

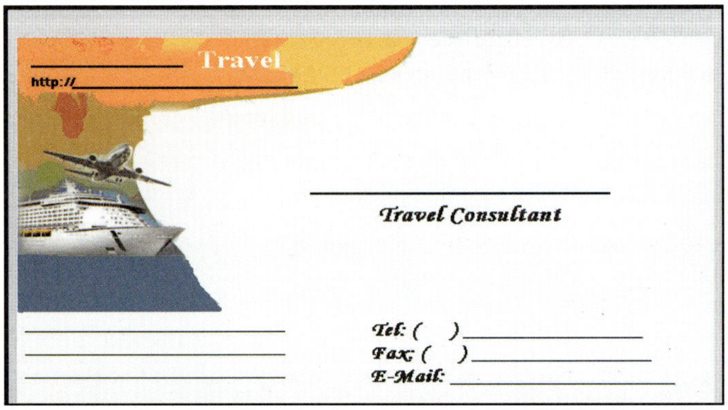

◆ **Look at the Sample Business Card on the right. Then write a Business Card for yourself.**

**You're going to call Ramada Hotel.**
**Fill out the information below.**

Your name: ______________________

Company: ______________________

Contact No. ______________________

You want to speak to: ______________________

Reasons for your call:

______________________________________

______________________________________

❑ **Who answered your call:** ______________

❑ **Why was the person unavailable:**

______________________________________

◆ **You work for Ramada Hotel.**
**Answer the phone and take a message.**

**Someone Called While You Were Out**

To: ______________ Date: ______________

From: ______________ Time: ______________

Of: ______________ Phone: ______________

❑ Will call again ❑ Please call

❑ Returned your call

**Message Box**

______________________________________

______________________________________

______________________________________

______________________________________

*Message taken by:* ______________

## 6-1 PAIR WORK

**STUDENT A**

| CONSULTANT | TOURIST |
|---|---|
| Good afternoon. What can I do for you? | I'd like to change my reservation, please. |
| Can I have your full name, please? | It's **Joe Waters**. |
| How do you spell that? | It's **J-O-E**. And my last name is **W-A-T-E-R-S**. |
| **J-O-E …W-A-T-E-R**. Is that correct? | No, it's **W-A-T-E-R-S**. |
| How can I change your reservation? | I want to change my **check-in /departure** to **March 30th**. |
| Is your contact number **516-738-4783**? | No, it isn't. It's **516-738-4738**. |
| Is there anything else I can help you with? | No, that's all. |
| Thanks for calling. Have a pleasant day! | Good-bye. |

**Part One:** You role-play the following TOURISTS.
Use the information below to change your Hotel Reservation.

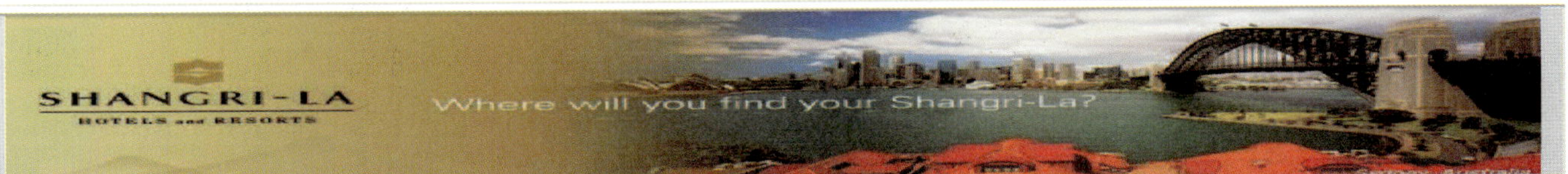


| NAME | CHECK-IN | CHECK-OUT | ROOM TYPE | CONTACT NO. |
|---|---|---|---|---|
| Mr. Jon Brown | May 2nd | May 8th | Double | 718-275-0925 |
| | | | | |
| Mrs. Sidney Smith | February 15th | February 18th | Honeymoon Suite | 716-462-0089 |

**Part Two:** You are a CONSULTANT. Write down the changes.

| NAME | DESTINATION | AIRLINE | DEPARTURE | CONTACT NO. |
|---|---|---|---|---|
| Mr. Jackie Chang | New Delhi | Air India | September 11th | 213-555-1936 |
| Mr. Jacky Chan | Buenos Aires | US Airways | July 15th | 852-923-6511 |
| Mrs. Clair Joel | Honolulu | Aloha Airline | December 23rd | 734-641-0007 |
| Mrs. Clare Joe | Anchorage | China Airline | August 2nd | 205-852-2020 |

## ⑥-2 PAIR WORK

**○ STUDENT B**

| CONSULTANT | TOURIST |
|---|---|
| Good afternoon. What can I do for you? | I'd like to change my reservation, please. |
| Can I have your full name, please? | It's **Joe Waters**. |
| How do you spell that? | It's **J-O-E**. And my last name is **W-A-T-E-R-S**. |
| **J-O-E … W-A-T-E-R**. Is that correct? | No, it's **W-A-T-E-R-S**. |
| How can I change your reservation? | I want to change my **check-in /departure** to **March 30th**. |
| Is your contact number **516-738-4783**? | No, it isn't. It's **516-738-4738**. |
| Is there anything else I can help you with? | No, that's all. |
| Thanks for calling. Have a pleasant day! | Good-bye. |

**Part One:** You are a CONSULTANT. Write down the changes.

| NAME | CHECK-IN | CHECK-OUT | ROOM TYPE | CONTACT NO. |
|---|---|---|---|---|
| Mr. Jon Browne | May 5th | May 8th | Double | 718-275-0952 |
| Mr. John Braun | October 28th | October 30th | Suite | 905-729-9854 |
| Mrs. Sidney Schmidt | February 14th | February 18th | Honeymoon Suite | 617-462-0089 |
| Mrs. Sydney Smith | April 4th | April 5th | Deluxe Twin | 469-345-2002 |

**Part Two:** You role-play the following TOURISTS.
Use the information below to change your Travel Reservation.

| NAME | DESTINATION | AIRLINE | DEPARTURE | CONTACT NO. |
|---|---|---|---|---|
| Mr. Jackie Chan | New Delhi | Air India | October 11th | 213-554-1936 |
| | | | | |
| Mrs. Clair Joe | Honolulu | Aloha Airline | December 3rd | 734-461-0007 |

## 7 READING

### Cell Phone Etiquette

1 Cell phones are everywhere nowadays, and many people don't know when to turn them off. How many times has a relaxing dinner out been disturbed by the diner at the next table whose cell phone rings? Or how about the long awaited climax of the suspense thriller that was ruined by the movie patron who forgot to turn off his cell phone?

2 Cell phones have become part of the urban landscape. Some businesses and public places have devised ways to deal with this technology. In New York, some restaurants have exclusive cell phone lounges. Other establishments have posted signs near their doors warning patrons to be courteous when it comes to talking on the wireless.

3 As cell phone use escalates, so does the call for some kind of wireless etiquette. Some basic cell phone etiquette rules include:

- Know when to turn your cell phone off, e.g. meetings, movies, worship, restaurants, classes, funerals, etc.
- Respect the personal space of others by taking your conversation 10 or more feet away from people.
- Be polite and don't scream. Speak in a lower than normal voice, you'll be heard by the caller.
- Do not interrupt a face-to-face conversation by answering your cell phone. The person you are actually with takes priority.

4 It is hard to imagine a world without cell phones. But it's time to shape up cell phone behavior before its use in public is restricted. Cell phone users could soon be treated like smokers. While this may sound exaggerated, minding our cell phone manners can only have a positive effect.

## COMPREHENSION

◆ **Write T if the sentence is true and F if the sentence is false. If it is false, make it true.**

**1.** Talking on the cell phone disturbs people. _____

**2.** Some movie theatres have sections for cell phone users. _____

**3.** Always speak loudly when using your cell phone. _____

**4.** You should turn off your cell phone in church, class, and restaurant. _____

**5.** It is polite to answer your cell phone when you're talking with your friend. _____

**6.** Cell phones may be restricted in public if we aren't more careful in using them. _____

## 8 ONE MORE TIME

◆ **The Host selects 2 Contestants, and 2 Panels – Each Panel consists of 6 members. The Host selects a question and reads it. The 2 Contestants and the Panel Members will circle their choice and the contestants will tell the Host. The Panel Members will tell the Host their answers. The Host will match the Contestants' answers to the Panels. For every match the contestant will receive 1 point. The Contestant with the most matches (after 4 rounds) gets to play a BONUS ROUND.**

PANEL MEMBERS

HOST

| ROUND 1 | ROUND 2 | ROUND 3 | ROUND 4 |
|---|---|---|---|
| **Mrs. Chow is _______.** | **Mr. Chan of ________ called.** | **Good morning. Grand Hyatt Hotel. _______** | **Cell Phone _______.** |
| a) busy<br>b) in a meeting<br>c) at lunch<br>d) on vacation<br>e) on a business trip | a) Pacific Travel<br>b) Fantasy Island<br>c) Seychelles Resorts<br>d) Orient Travel<br>e) Uni Tours | a) Sandra speaking.<br>b) May I help you?<br>c) How can I help you?<br>d) What can I do for you?<br>e) How may I direct your call? | a) disturbs people<br>b) is very useful<br>c) can cause traffic accidents<br>d) is a symbol of social status<br>e) has become part of our lives. |
| **Points For Contestants:** | **Points For Contestants:** | **Points For Contestants:** | **Points For Contestants:** |
| **C1.** ________<br>**C2.** ________ | **C1.** ________<br>**C2.** ________ | **C1.** ________<br>**C2.** ________ | **C1.** ________<br>**C2.** ________ |

**STRUCTURE:**

**H:** Contestants, Panel Members …
Are you ready to match?
**C/PM:** Yes, we are ready.
**H:** (Reads **Question 1** … )
**Contestant A**, which Panel do you want?
**CA:** I'll go with **Panel B.**
**H:** What's your answer?
**CA:** My answer is **E**.
**H:** Panel Members, what are your answers?
**P:** I chose (**E/C/D/A/E/B**)
**H:** **Contestant A**, you've matched **2 members**. You receive **2 points**. You've got the most matches. It's time to go to the Bonus Round!

**BONUS ROUND**

**Q: In which country are cell phones most popular?**

**STRUCTURE:**

**H:** Choose 4 Panel Members to help you choose the correct answer.
**C:** I choose **Joel, Cindy, Paul and Veronica**.
**H:** **Joel, Cindy, Paul, and Veronica** …
What's your answer?
**PM:** My answer is **Canada**.
**H:** Contestant, choose 1 of these answers or your own.
**C:** I'll go with **Canada**.
**H: Sorry, that's incorrect.**

# Chapter 2

*Crossing The Border.*

## ❶ KEY VOCABULARY

| | | | |
|---|---|---|---|
| Concierge | Tour Conductor | Bus Boy | Chef |
| Cabin Crew | Chauffeur | Event Planner | Pilot |
| Maitre d' | Dealer | Masseuse | Immigration Officer |
| Purser | Doorman | Chambermaid | Caddie |
| GRO | Ground Crew | Lifeguard | Cashier |
| Bellboy | Valet | Receptionist | Server |

## ❷ WARM-UP

A ____________

B ____________

C ____________

D ____________

E ____________

F ____________

G ____________

H ____________

### Can You Guess Who I Am?

**Fill in the occupation under the picture.**

◆ **Make groups of three. The leader chooses one picture and describes the picture to the group. The members will try to guess what picture it is.**

**DAILY RESPONSIBILITIES: (Hints)**

◆ **collect money** ◆ **help servers**
◆ **carry bags** ◆ **drive a limousine**
◆ **rescue swimmers** ◆ **fly an airplane**
◆ **am in charge of the cabin crew**
◆ **provide special services to guests**

**STRUCTURE:**

**Leader:** Are you ready?
**Students:** Yes, we are ready.
**Leader:** Everyday I **carry golf clubs**.
**Student B:** Where do you work?
**Leader:** I work **in a country club**. Who am I?
**Student A:** Are you **a bell boy**?
**Leader:** No, I'm not. Try again!
**Student B:** I know. Are you **a Caddie**?
**Leader:** Yes, I am. It's your turn now.

## ❸ LANGUAGE STRUCTURE

| QUESTIONS | ANSWERS |
|---|---|
| What is your nationality? | I am Chinese. |
| Where are you from? | I am from Britain. |
| Why do you want to go to the United States? | I want to see Las Vegas. |
| How do you spell your surname? | It's S-P-I-E-L-B-E-R-G. |
| Which country do you want to visit? | I want to visit Australia. |
| How much does it cost? | It costs $1,050. |
| Who is your favorite actor/actress? | My favorite actress is Julia Roberts. |
| How long will you be staying here? | I'll be staying for a week. |

➢ **Write the questions. Use these words below and then answer the questions.**

| Who | What | Where | When | How | Why | Which |
|---|---|---|---|---|---|---|

| | | |
|---|---|---|
| **1.** | **How** often do you travel? | I ____ travel. (often, seldom, always, never) |
| **2.** | ________ do you want to be? | I want to be a(an) ______________________. |
| **3.** | ________ do you want to go for vacation? | I want to go to ______________________. |
| **4.** | ________ do you want to go to there? | I want to see the ______________________. |
| **5.** | ________ are you entering this country? | I'm entering for ______________________. |
| **6.** | ________ airline do you prefer? | I prefer ______________________. |
| **7.** | ________ is the most famous Korean? | I think the most famous Korean is ________. |

➢ **Walk around the classroom. Ask your classmates the above questions and write down their answers.**

| Name | Q1 | Q2 | Q3 | Q4 | Q5 | Q6 | Q7 |
|---|---|---|---|---|---|---|---|
| | | | | | | | |
| | | | | | | | |
| | | | | | | | |
| | | | | | | | |
| | | | | | | | |

## ❹ CONVERSATION

➢ **Practice the following dialogue with a partner.**

**Woman:** Great party! What's your name?
**Man:** My name's **Claude.** ❶
**Woman:** How do you spell your first name?
**Man:** It's **C-L-A-U-D-E**. ❷
**Woman:** Oh my gosh!!! I love your accent. Are you from **France**? ①
**Man:** No, I'm from Canada. You have such a beautiful voice! What's your nationality?
**Woman:** I'm **Hungarian**. ②
**Man:** That's cool. How long have you been in this country?
**Woman:** I've been here a few hours. So, **what do you do, Claude**? ③
**Man:** I'm a **pilot for Scandinavian Airline**. ❸
**Woman:** I can't believe it! I also work for **Scandinavian Airline**. ④ I'm a **flight attendant**. ⑤
**Man:** It's a small world. How long have you been working for the **airline**? ❹
**Woman:** I just started last month. Um, it's very hot and noisy here.
**Man:** Yes, it's really stuffy. How about taking a walk outside?
**Woman:** Okay, that sounds great!

## SUBSTITUTION DRILL

➢ **Substitute with the words or phrases below:**

| Man | Woman |
|---|---|
| ❶ Ivan<br>Charles<br>Kamal | ① Russia<br>England<br>India |
| ❷ I-V-A-N<br>C-H-A-R-L-E-S<br>K-A-M-A-L | ② German<br>Swedish<br>Czech |
| ❸ dealer for Caesars Casino<br>concierge for London Hilton Hotel<br>maitre d' for Tavern On The Green | ③ what do you do for a living, Ivan<br>what's your occupation, Charles<br>how do you make ends meet, Kamal |
| ❹ casino<br>hotel<br>restaurant | ④ Caesars Casino<br>London Hilton Hotel<br>Tavern On The Green |
| | ⑤ server<br>G.R.O.<br>Bartender |

## 5 CHALLENGE YOURSELF

➤ **Matching**

| COUNTRY | | CAPITAL CITY | | NATIONALITY | | LANGUAGE |
|---|---|---|---|---|---|---|
| _____ Vietnam | A | Ankara | 1 | Singaporean | O | Mongolian |
| _____ Austria | B | New Delhi | 2 | Israeli | P | Swahili |
| _____ Italy | C | Jerusalem | 3 | Brazilian | Q | Vietnamese |
| _____ Ireland | D | Singapore | 4 | Austrian | R | Divehi |
| _____ Maldives | E | Hanoi | 5 | Turkish | S | Hebrew |
| _____ Israel | F | Nairobi | 6 | Indian | T | Chinese |
| _____ Mongolia | G | Rome | 7 | Vietnamese | U | Portuguese |
| _____ Kenya | H | Dublin | 8 | Maldivian | V | Italian |
| _____ Brazil | I | Vienna | 9 | Irish | W | Turkish |
| _____ Turkey | J | Brasilia | 10 | Mongolian | X | German |
| _____ Singapore | K | Male | 11 | Kenyan | Y | Bengali |
| _____ India | L | Ulaanbaatar | 12 | Italian | Z | English |

➤ **Use the words below to fill in the chart.**

| WORKPLACE | RESPONSIBILITIES |
|---|---|
| ◆ hotel ◆ restaurant ◆ airport ◆ airline ◆ casino ◆ country resorts/clubs | ◆ hands out cards ◆ helps servers ◆ carries golf clubs ◆ massages people ◆ is in charge of the cabin crew ◆ parks cars ◆ is a head waiter ◆ opens doors ◆ prepares food ◆ collects boarding passes ◆ flies an airplane ◆ cleans rooms |

| S/He is a … | S/He works in a/an … | S/He … |
|---|---|---|
| **1.** masseuse ➲ | | |
| **2.** maitre d' ➲ | | |
| **3.** doorman ➲ | | |
| **4.** chef ➲ | | |
| **5.** dealer ➲ | | |
| **6.** ground crew ➲ | | |
| **7.** pilot ➲ | | |
| **8.** bus boy ➲ | | |
| **9.** chambermaid ➲ | | |
| **10.** valet ➲ | | |
| **11.** caddie ➲ | | |
| **12.** purser ➲ | | |

## ❻-1 PAIR WORK

**○ STUDENT A**

| QUESTIONS | ANSWERS |
|---|---|
| 1. Where is **Sandra** from? | **She** is from **Sweden**. |
| 2. What is **her** nationality? | **Her** nationality is **Swedish**. |
| 3. What language does **she** speak? | **She** speaks **Swedish**. |
| 4. What does **she** do? | **She** is a(an) **event planner**. |

◆ **Ask STUDENT B for the information you need.**

| NAME | COUNTRY | NATIONALITY | LANGUAGE | OCCUPATION |
|---|---|---|---|---|
|  **Yvonne** | | | | |
|  **Luigi** | Italy | Italian | Italian | Immigration Officer |
|  **Lin** | | | | |
|  **Josef** | Morocco | Moroccan | Arabic | Chef |
|  **Petra** | | | | |
|  **Hans** | South Africa | South African | English | Tour guide |

## ⑥-2 PAIR WORK

**STUDENT B**

| QUESTIONS | ANSWERS |
| --- | --- |
| 1. Where is **Sandra** from? | **She** is from **Sweden**. |
| 2. What is **her** nationality? | **Her** nationality is **Swedish**. |
| 3. What language does **she** speak? | **She** speaks **Swedish**. |
| 4. What does **she** do? | **She** is a(an) **event planner**. |

◆ **Ask STUDENT A for the information you need.**

| NAME | COUNTRY | NATIONALITY | LANGUAGE | OCCUPATION |
| --- | --- | --- | --- | --- |
|  **Yvonne** | Russia | Russian | Russian | Co-pilot |
|  **Luigi** | | | | |
|  **Lin** | Japan | Japanese | Japanese | Event Planner |
|  **Josef** | | | | |
|  **Petra** | Germany | German | German | Ground Crew |
|  **Hans** | | | | |

## 7 READING

### The Mystique Of The Flight Attendant

1 The job of a flight attendant is considered to be glamorous, sexy, adventurous and exciting. The mere mention of the flight attendant job conjures up images of jetting away to exotic places or spending a week in Europe shopping or skiing.

2 Initially the first cabin attendants were men known as couriers. By the late 1930's female attendants or stewardess were hired. Up to the 1940's these stewardesses were registered nurses. Their main duties were to hand out sandwiches and attend those who got sick. In those days the airplanes were very noisy and not as comfortable. In the 1940's the job was considered to be glamorous. Many young women wanted to become airline stewardesses but only a few were chosen. When stewardesses got married, they were terminated. By the 1960's men were on the job. As a result of an influx of males the job title of flight attendant was created.

3 The job of a flight attendant is in reality hard work. It is difficult to find the glamour in this job when you are looking for someone's dentures they left on a tray! Working a 14-hour day due to a mechanical delay and dealing with a planeload of airsick passengers during heavy turbulence can be challenging.

4 Possibly the most important component of the mystery surrounding the flight attendant is the fact that it is a difficult job to get. Less than 10% of those who apply are selected for the job.

5 No other jobs satisfy the fantasy of world travel quite as flying. How many other jobs offer the benefits, excitement and prestige than flying does, not to mention the shopping and sightseeing!!

### COMPREHENSION

◆ **One word in each sentence is incorrect. Cross it out and write the correct answer.**

**1.** The first cabin attendants were females.

**2.** At the beginning stewardesses were models.

**3.** Men became flight attendants in the 1970's.

**4.** Airlines accept most of their applicants.

**5.** Stewardesses were encouraged to get married.

**6.** A flight attendant's job is adventurous, glamorous, easy and exciting.

## 8 ONE MORE TIME

### Part One:

**INSTRUCTIONS:**

- Make groups of 4. 2 students are X; and 2 students are O.

1. If the questioning team asks a grammatically correct question; and the answering team answers it grammatically correct – then 1 student from each team will do rock, paper, scissors. The winner gets an X or O for his/her team.
2. If the questioning team asks a grammatically incorrect question; the other team will get an X or O if they can come up with a grammatically correct question.
3. If the questioning team asks a grammatically correct question; and the other team answers it incorrectly – then the questioning team gets an X or O if they can answer it correctly.

**EXAMPLE:**

1. **Question Team:** Why were you late for class today? **Answer Team:** I was late because I overslept. (Both teams are correct; 1 student from each team will do rock, paper, scissors – the winner gets an X or O.)
2. **Question Team:** Why were late you today class for? **Answer Team:** Why were you late for class today? (The Question Team makes an incorrect question; the Answer Team makes the question correctly – the Answer Team gets an X or O.)
3. **Question Team:** Why were you late for class today? **Answer Team:** I was late because overslept. (The question is correct; but the answer is incorrect – the Question Team gets an X or O if they can answer it correctly.)

**TIC TAC TOE CARD 1**

| | | |
|---|---|---|
| When...? | What...? | How...? |
| Who...? | How long...? | Where...? |
| Which...? | How many...? | Why...? |

### Part Two:

- Using the same groups. One group will pick a square. The other group will ask the following questions.

**STRUCTURE:**

**Team A:** S/He **prepares food**. Who is s/he?
**Team B:** S/He is **a cook**. (Team B gets an X or O)

- If the answer is wrong, team A gets an X or O.

**TIC TAC TOE CARD 2**

| | | |
|---|---|---|
| Event Planner | Chauffer | Caddie |
| Bus boy | Concierge | Cashier |
| Valet | Immigration Officer | Dealer |

# Chapter 3

## *Don't Miss Your Flight!*

## ❶ KEY VOCABULARY

| | | | |
|---|---|---|---|
| A quarter to | Once a week | Every other day | Half past |
| ETD | Midnight | Noon | Mid-day |
| Local Time | Ahead of schedule | Daily | Cancelled |
| Every hour on the hour | Eight oh five | Every hour on the half hour | Every half an hour |
| Delayed | Twenty to … | ETA | Hourly |
| Biweekly | Weekly | Fifteen after | Postpone |

## ❷ WARM-UP

➢ **Fill in the blanks using the vocabulary above.**

**A.** The train to Pusan leaves ___________.
The train to Seoul leaves _____________.

| KTX to Pusan | KTX to Seoul |
|---|---|
| KTX | KTX |
| 8:30 | 9:00 |
| 9:30 | 10:00 |
| 10:30 | 11:00 |
| 11:30 | 12:00 |

**B.** Cebu Pacific has a ___________ flight to Manila.

| Cebu Pacific To Manila | Monday Only. |
|---|---|

**C.** The _____________ of UA 884 is 13:25.
UA 800 is ________________.

ARRIVALS

| United Airline | From | Arrival |
|---|---|---|
| **Flight** | | |
| UA 884 | Chicago | 13:25 |
| UA 800 | Tokyo | 11:45 ⇨ 11:15 |

**D.** The ____________ of CA 126 is 19:30.
CA 144 is ________________.

DEPARURES

| Air China | To | Departure |
|---|---|---|
| **Flight** | | |
| CA 126 | Beijing | 19:30 |
| CA 144 | Yanji | 15:10 ⇨ 22:50 |

## ❸ LANGUAGE STRUCTURE

| QUESTIONS | ANSWERS |
|---|---|
| What time does your flight depart? | It departs at half past nine. |
| What time does your flight arrive? | It arrives at twenty one forty-five. |
| How much is the airfare? | It's $330 plus taxes. |
| When are you picking up the ticket? | I'll get it on February $15^{th}$. |

**Part One:**

It's ________ fifteen.
It's a quarter after __________.
It's fifteen past ___________.

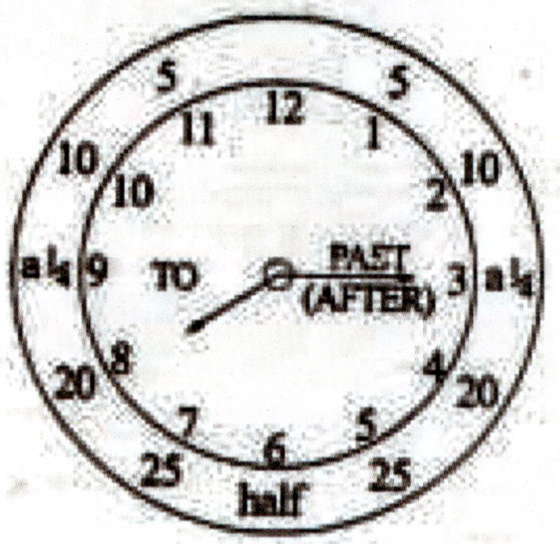


➢ **Listen to your teacher. Draw the hands on the clock and write the times in words.**

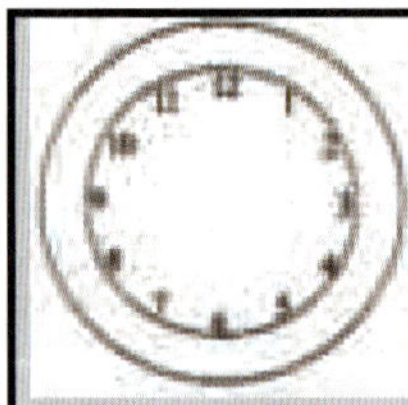
1
________________
________________
________________

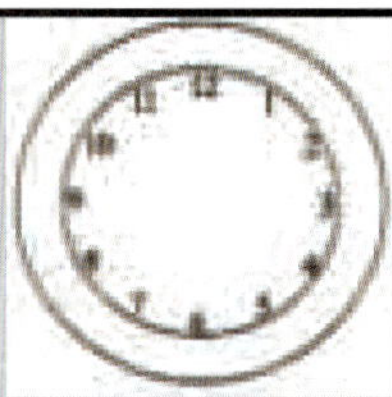
2
________________
________________
________________

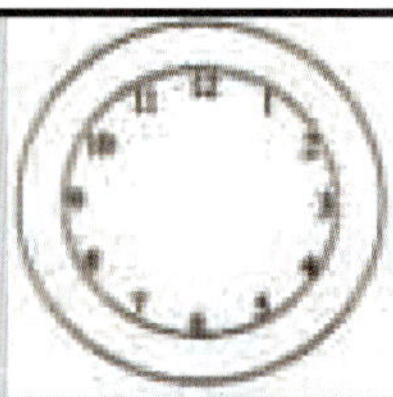
3
________________
________________
________________

**Part Two:**

**Reading numbers in English is easy if you know the basic system. It is divided into ones, tens, hundreds, thousands, billions, trillions and zillions.**

| 1 | ,000 | ,000 | ,000 | ,000 | ,000 |
|---|---|---|---|---|---|
| | **Zillion** | **Trillion** | **Billion** | **Million** | **Thousand** |

**A.** 63, 972: ________________________________________.
**B.** 10, 923, 789: ________________________________________.
**C.** 33, 177, 656, 007: ________________________________________.
**D.** One million two hundred and fifty thousand: ________________________________________.
**E.** Five hundred seventy thousand two hundred and eleven: ________________________________________.
**F.** Seven billion one hundred million six hundred and sixty-six thousand: ________________________________________.

## ❹ CONVERSATION

➢ **Practice the following dialogue with a partner.**

**Robert:** What are you doing this summer vacation?
**Laura:** I'm going to **Italy**. And what about you? ①
**Robert:** Nothing much.
**Laura:** Do you want to come with me?
**Robert:** I wish I could, but I think the **airfare** is really expensive. ❶
**Laura:** Not really. It's only $**760**. ②
**Robert:** That's **cheap**! I think I can afford it. ❷
**Laura:** So are we going to **Rome** together? ③
**Robert:** Of course, we are. When are you **picking up** the ticket? ❸
**Laura:** I'll be at the travel agency this Saturday at **a quarter past two**. ④
**Robert:** Oh, I have to work this Saturday. Will you buy the ticket for me?

## SUBSTITUTION DRILL

➢ **Substitute with the words or phrases below:**

| Laura | Robert |
|---|---|
| ① the Maldives<br>Egypt<br>Turkey | ❶ flight<br>ticket<br>fare |
| ② 830<br>915<br>616 | ❷ inexpensive<br>a bargain<br>a good deal |
| ③ Male<br>Cairo<br>Istanbul | ❸ buying<br>purchasing<br>getting |
| ④ a quarter to ten<br>half past twelve<br>noon | |

## ❺ CHALLENGE YOURSELF

**Part One:** ➢ **Match the letters (A-L) with the numbers (1-12).**

| | | ANSWERS |
|---|---|---|
| **A.** A quarter to ten P.M. | **1.** 12:00 | A ________ |
| **B.** Five past one in the morning | **2.** 07:20 | B ________ |
| **C.** Twenty to nine in the evening | **3.** 08:30 | C ________ |
| **D.** Midnight | **4.** 18:55 | D ________ |
| **E.** Twenty past seven in the morning | **5.** 14:15 | E ________ |
| **F.** Ten past three in the afternoon | **6.** 01:05 | F ________ |
| **G.** Twenty-five to eleven at night | **7.** 23:00 | G ________ |
| **H.** Five to seven in the evening | **8.** 20:40 | H ________ |
| **I.** Half past eight A.M. | **9.** 00:00 | I ________ |
| **J.** Noon | **10.** 22:35 | J ________ |
| **K.** A quarter past two in the afternoon | **11.** 15:10 | K ________ |
| **L.** Eleven at night | **12.** 21:45 | L ________ |

**Part Two:** ➢ **What floor am I on?**

◆ **SCENARIO:**
**A friend of yours is lost in a hundred floors building. Can you find your friend?**

☑ **Work in groups of four. The leader goes first and writes down a number from 1 to 100. The other students will have 10 chances to guess what floor the leader is on.**

**STRUCTURE:**

**Student A:** Are you on the **56th** floor?
**Leader:** No. You should go **higher**.
**Student B:** Are you on the **85th** floor?
**Leader:** No. You must go **lower**.
**Student D:** Are you on the **73rd** floor?
**Leader:** No. You must go **higher**.
**Student A:** Are you on the **75th** floor?
**Leader:** No. You must go **lower**.
**Student B:** Are you on the **74th** floor?
**Leader:** Yes, I am.

◆ **Student B gets to choose a floor. Then repeat the activity.**

**Taipei 101**, Taiwan
The world's tallest building

**Petronas Towers**
Kuala Lumpur, Malaysia

**Empire State Building**
New York City

## ❻-1 PAIR WORK

**O STUDENT A**

**Part One:** **Read the following airline announcement to your partner.**

1. This is the final call for Air Canada's flight AC 266 to Montreal, which departs at 20:35. Would passengers please proceed to gate 60A at once. The ETA of flight AC 266 is 23:09 local time.

2. Last call for Lufthansa's flight LH 853 to Frankfurt. The 20:18 departure to Frankfurt is now boarding at Gate 50. The flight is now boarding. The ETA of flight LH 853 is 20:17.

3. Flight TG 350 bound for Bangkok will be departing from Gate 17 at 18:08. This is the first announcement of Thai International flight TG 350. The ETA of flight TG 350 is 02:20 local time.

**Part Two:** **Listen to the airline announcement and fill in the chart.**
**If you want STUDENT B to repeat it say "Please repeat it".**

| Airline | Flight Number | Destination | Gate Number | ETA |
|---|---|---|---|---|
| CATHAY PACIFIC | | | | |
| nwa NORTHWEST AIRLINES | | | | |
| BRITISH AIRWAYS | | | | |

## ⑥-2 PAIR WORK

**○ STUDENT B**

**Part One:** **Listen to the airline announcement and fill in the chart.**
**If you want STUDENT A to repeat it say "<u>Please repeat it</u>".**

| Airline | Flight Number | Destination | Gate Number | ETA |
|---|---|---|---|---|
| AIR CANADA | | | | |
| Lufthansa | | | | |
| Thai | | | | |

**Part Two:** **Read the following airline announcement to your partner.**

1. All passengers leaving on the 21:16 flight to Tokyo on Cathay Pacific CX 304 should be at Gate 58 for immediate boarding. The flight is now boarding. The ETA of flight CX 304 is 03:20

2. Would all passengers heading for Chicago go immediately to Gate 14 for the 11:40 departure of Northwest Airline's flight NW 215. The ETA of NW 215 is 18:13.

3. British Airways Flight BA 711 bound for Paris is now boarding at Gate 12. The flight will depart at 15:57 after a slight delay. The ETA of BA 711 is 19:24 local time.

## 7 READING

# Jetlag

1 If you travel enough, sooner or later you will fall victim to the ever-popular traveling syndrome known as jetlag. It is the feeling of lack of energy, weird sleeping patterns and always feeling tired. Jet lag occurs when a traveler passes over a number of time zones that disrupt the normal sleeping rhythm. Some say it's caused by dehydration from the airplane trip, altitude sickness or lack of sleep. While all of these may be true, the one definite factor is the change in sleeping patterns. You arrive in Italy and it may be 1 o'clock in the afternoon, but your body insists that it is 3 in the morning.

2 Other factors include the stale cabin air, lack of exercise or movement, your current health, and the worrying and anticipation of the trip. While traveling may be a wondrous occasion, it can be quite a stressful one as well.

3 Jetlag tends to be more severe traveling from west to east as you are losing time, while east to west is less severe because you are gaining time.

4 Some tips to prevent jetlag are:

- Try to get some sleep on the plane. You'd be surprised how many people force themselves to stay awake for the movie.
- Limit your alcohol, coffee and sleeping pills intake.
- Drink a lot of water. Try to hydrate (water) yourself more than the flight dehydrates you.
- Take supplemental vitamins before, during, and after your trip. Melatonin and zinc have had reportedly good results for jetlag. Eat lots of vegetables.
- When you arrive try to adapt to the new time of day immediately. For example, force yourself to stay awake until the time of day you would normally go to sleep back home.
- Get up and stretch. Break it up a bit, instead of ringing your call button; come get a drink in the back.

5 So the next time you are on a long plane trip, follow these simple tips and you should arrive at your destination in better shape. Bon Voyage and sweet dreams!!!

## COMPREHENSION

◆ **Answer the questions using complete sentences.**

**1.** What is jetlag?

**2.** What are some factors that cause jetlag?

**3.** Why does jetlag happen?

**4.** Name at least 4 things you should do on the airplane to prevent jetlag.

**5.** What factor may increase the chance of you getting jetlag?

## 8 ONE MORE TIME

☑ Choose 24 times.
Fill out the Bingo Card. ➔

| | |
|---|---|
| 3:05 | 12:00 PM |
| 11:15 | 23:50 |
| 03:18 | 2:15 |
| 20:20 | 19:10 |
| 12:00 AM | 5:55 |
| 7:10 | 1:30 |
| 22:40 | 6:45 |
| 18:55 | 00:25 |
| 9:13 | 22:50 |
| 23:30 | 19:30 |
| 6:35 | 5:45 |
| 13:40 | 9:55 |
| 11:50 | 15:15 |
| 8:30 | 18:40 |
| 20:00 | 10:10 |

Listen to your teacher call out a time. When you hear the time on your Bingo Card called out, cross it out (X).

**BINGO CARD 1**

| B | I | N | G | O |
|---|---|---|---|---|
| | | | | |
| | | | | |
| | | FREE | | |
| | | | | |
| | | | | |

☑ Choose 24 numbers.
Fill out the Bingo Card. ➔

| | |
|---|---|
| 13 | 55,920 |
| 940,900 | 3,313 |
| 516 | 30 |
| 188,230 | 130,430 |
| 716 | 760 |
| 17,770 | 17,000 |
| 118,230 | 916,900 |
| 12 | 70,000 |
| 18,818 | 130,413 |
| 560 | 3,330 |
| 113,340 | 960,900 |
| 20 | 8,600,014 |
| 8,600,040 | 40 |
| 1,625,215 | 1,625,250 |
| 18,880 | 55,912 |

Listen to your teacher call out the number. When you hear the number on your Bingo Card called out, cross it out (X).

**BINGO CARD 2**

| B | I | N | G | O |
|---|---|---|---|---|
| | | | | |
| | | | | |
| | | FREE | | |
| | | | | |
| | | | | |

# Chapter 4

## *The Pyramids Are Older Than Angkor Wat.*

## ❶ KEY VOCABULARY

| | | | |
|---|---|---|---|
| Banquet | Crowded | Exciting | Interesting |
| Safe | Satellite TV | Convenient | Babysitting Service |
| Facilities | Challenging | Conference | Fast |
| Luxurious | City Center | Handicap | Balcony |
| Shuttle Bus | Boring | Relaxing | Romantic |
| Noisy | Mini-bar | In-room safe | Laundry |

## ❷ WARM-UP

**Part One:**

◆ **Write down what you think the following symbols mean.**

A ____________

B ____________

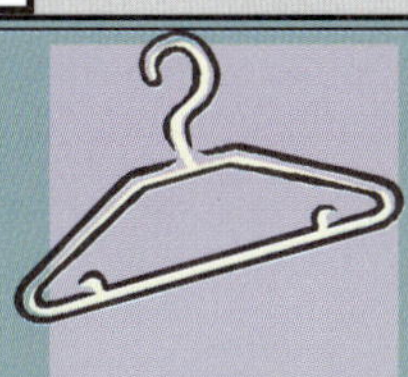

C ____________

D ____________

E ____________

F ____________

**Part Two:**

◆ **Draw symbols for the following:**

| Immigration | Information |
|---|---|
| | |
| **Shuttle Bus** | **Satellite TV** |
| | |

➢ **Compare your symbols with a partner. Decide which one is better.**

## ❸ LANGUAGE STRUCTURE

### Comparatives

A way to compare two things or people is by adding **-er** to the end of the adjectives; or by using **more** in front of the adjectives. We also must use **than** after the adjectives.

**Example:**

**A:** W Hotel has 253 rooms.
Lotte Hotel has 1, 479 rooms. ⇨ W Hotel is **smaller than** Lotte Hotel.

**B:** The airfare to Jeju-do is W170, 000.
The airfare to Daegu is W115, 000. ⇨ The airfare to Jeju-do is **more expensive than** the airfare to Daegu.

| | Adjective | Comparative |
|---|---|---|
| Add **-er** to one-syllable adjectives. | fast ⇨<br>safe | fast**er than**<br>saf**er than** |
| Adjectives that end in **–y**, change the **-y** to **i** and add **–er**. | noisy ⇨<br>pretty | nois**ier than**<br>prett**ier than** |
| Adjectives with two or more syllables use more in front of it, except adjectives that end in **–y**. | luxurious ⇨<br>exciting<br>comfortable | **more** luxurious **than**<br>**more** exciting **than**<br>**more** comfortable **than** |
| **Exceptions:**<br>The comparative forms of good, bad, and far are irregular. | good ⇨<br>bad<br>far | better **than**<br>worse **than**<br>farther/further **than** |

❑ **Write a comparative sentence using the following words.**

**1.** crowded: ____________________
**2.** luxurious: ____________________
**3.** far: ____________________
**4.** expensive: ____________________
**5.** romantic: ____________________
**6.** exciting: ____________________
**7.** relaxing: ____________________
**8.** noisy: ____________________
**9.** dangerous: ____________________
**10.** good: ____________________
**11.** old: ____________________
**12.** cheap: ____________________
**13.** big: ____________________
**14.** hot: ____________________
**15.** dry: ____________________
**16.** heavy: ____________________

## ❹ CONVERSATION

➤ **Practice the following dialogue with a partner.**

**Shawn:** Where **should we** go on our honeymoon? ❶
**Barbara:** I'd love to go to Paris. It is so **romantic**. ①
**Shawn:** Yes, it is. But it's **more expensive** than Jeju-do. ❷
**Barbara:** Jeju-do is **cheaper**, but a safari in Africa would be more exciting. ②
**Shawn:** Why don't we go to Pattaya. It's **closer** and romantic. ❸
**Barbara:** Yes, but I think it's **more crowded** than the Maldives. ③
**Shawn:** I know … let's go to Beijing.
**Barbara:** Beijing!? You must be joking? It's too cold **this time of year**. ④
**Shawn:** Yes, I know. But it's **more exciting** and cheaper than the Maldives. ❹
**Barbara:** Alright!!! If you want to go to Beijing, you can go by yourself.

## SUBSTITUTION DRILL

➤ **Substitute with the words or phrases below:**

| Shawn | Barbara |
|---|---|
| ❶ do you want to<br>will we<br>is the best place to | ① classy<br>intimate<br>charming |
| ❷ dearer<br>costlier<br>pricier | ② inexpensive<br>a good deal<br>less expensive |
| ❸ nearer<br>close by<br>not too far | ③ noisier<br>less romantic<br>less attractive |
| ❹ more interesting<br>bigger<br>closer | ④ in January<br>in the winter<br>right now |

## ❺ CHALLENGE YOURSELF

| | | | |
|---|---|---|---|
| close | small | dangerous | challenging |
| relaxing | boring | cheap | crowded |
| interesting | romantic | easy | quiet |
| expensive | noisy | hot | exciting |
| big | cold | slow | exotic |
| hard | thrilling | fun | entertaining |
| convenient | quick | attractive | comfortable |
| luxurious | charming | safe | famous |

**Part One:** **Compare the following using the words above.**

**EXAMPLE:** Prague / Kuala Lumpur: Prague is **more romantic than** Kuala Lumpur.
The airfare to Kuala Lumpur is **cheaper than** the airfare to Prague.

**1.**being a tour guide / being a stewardess: ______________________________.
**2.**China / Korea: ______________________________.
**3.**going to a casino / going to a museum: ______________________________.
**4.**English / Japanese: ______________________________.
**5.**flying / driving a car: ______________________________.
**6.**bungee jumping / swimming: ______________________________.
**7.**Bali / Moscow: ______________________________.
**8.**resorts / city hotels: ______________________________.

**Part Two:** **Find someone who has a different answer. Record his/her answer and name.**

**STRUCTURE:**

**Student A:** Excuse me. What do you have for number **1**?
**Student B:** Number **1** is: I think **being a tour guide** is **more exciting** than **being a stewardess**. And what do you think?
**Student A:** My answer is **different from** yours. I think **being a stewardess** is **more dangerous** than **being a tour guide**.
**Student B:** Okay. Our answers are **different**. Can I have your name, please?
**Student A:** Sure. My name is **Steven Halls**.

| Name: | Answer: |
|---|---|
| 1. ____________ | ______________________________ |
| 2. ____________ | ______________________________ |
| 3. ____________ | ______________________________ |
| 4. ____________ | ______________________________ |
| 5. ____________ | ______________________________ |
| 6. ____________ | ______________________________ |
| 7. ____________ | ______________________________ |
| 8. ____________ | ______________________________ |

## 6-1 PAIR WORK

**STUDENT**

| QUESTIONS | ANSWERS |
|---|---|
| Which is bigger, Lotte Hotel or W Hotel? | Lotte Hotel is bigger. It has 479 rooms. |
| Which is cheaper? | Lotte Hotel is cheaper. It costs $225 per night. |
| Which is more luxurious? | W Hotel is more luxurious. It is a 5 star hotel. |
| Which has more restaurants? | Lotte Hotel has more restaurants. It has 6 restaurants. |
| Which is closer to the city center? | Lotte Hotel is closer. It is in the city center. |

**Part One:** Look at the information below and answer STUDENT B's questions.

Caesars Palace Hotel

Excalibur Hotel

| | Caesars Palace Hotel | Excalibur Hotel |
|---|---|---|
| Number of rooms | 2,399 | 4,088 |
| Price per night | $250/night | $150/night |
| Luxury | 41/2 * | 3* |
| Number of restaurants | 10 | 5 |
| Distance from the city | City center | 1.6 kilometers from the city |

**Part Two:** Ask STUDENT B the above questions and fill in the chart below.

Burj Al Arab Hotel

Traders Hotel Dubai

| | Burj Al Arab Hotel | Traders Hotel Dubai |
|---|---|---|
| Bigger | | |
| Cheaper | | |
| More luxurious | | |
| More restaurants | | |
| Closer to the city | | |

## ⑥-2 PAIR WORK

**STUDENT B**

| QUESTIONS | ANSWERS |
|---|---|
| Which is bigger, Lotte Hotel or W Hotel? | Lotte Hotel is bigger. It has 479 rooms. |
| Which is cheaper? | Lotte Hotel is cheaper. It costs $225 per night. |
| Which is more luxurious? | W Hotel is more luxurious. It is a 5 star hotel. |
| Which has more restaurants? | Lotte Hotel has more restaurants. It has 6 restaurants. |
| Which is closer to the city center? | Lotte Hotel is closer. It is in the city center. |

**Part One:** Ask STUDENT A the above questions and fill in the chart below.

Caesars Palace Hotel

Excalibur Hotel

| | Caesars Palace Hotel | Excalibur Hotel |
|---|---|---|
| Smaller | | |
| More expensive | | |
| Less luxurious | | |
| Fewer restaurants | | |
| Further from the city center | | |

**Part Two:** Look at the information below and answer STUDENT A's questions.

Burj Al Arab Hotel

Traders Hotel Dubai

| | Burj Al Arab Hotel | Traders Hotel Dubai |
|---|---|---|
| Number of rooms | 202 | 259 |
| Price per night | $1,100 | $190 |
| Luxury | 5* | 4* |
| Number of restaurants | 6 | 2 |
| Distance from the city | 15 kilometers from the city | 4 kilometers from the city |

## 7 READING

### Angkor Wat: The Lost City

1 **F**or many travelers, the 'lost city' of Angkor is the reason for visiting Cambodia. Considering that the Kingdom of Angkor is one of the greatest wonders of the ancient world, it's not hard to understand why.

2 Angkor Wat is an architectural masterpiece. Angkor is the site where Khmer kings established their capitals from the ninth to the twelfth century. The civilization was highly developed as demonstrated by its temples and sculptures. It was constructed in the jungle in the early 12th century. Then, two centuries later, was mysteriously abandoned by the Khmer civilization. The jungle soon overwhelmed Angkor Wat, hiding it for several centuries with thick tropical foliage. There was little left to see except an occasional protruding building stone. In 1861 a French naturalist accidentally came across the ruins. Eventually archaeologists reclaimed Angkor Wat, exposing its magnificence.

3 Today, Angkor is a big archaeological site covering more than 400-square kilometers. More than 100 temples can be seen there.

4 The archaeological site includes many treasures. The most beautiful is the Hindu temple of Angkor Wat. It was constructed during the first half of twelfth century. Visitors are amazed at the building's details and exquisite stone carvings. Particularly interesting are the dancing female ("apsaras") sculptures decorating Angkor Wat.

## COMPREHENSION

◆ **Circle the correct answer.**

**1.** Angkor Wat is located in …
a) Vietnam b) Thailand c) Cambodia d) Laos

**2.** Angkor Wat was built in the …
a) city b) dessert c) forest d) jungle

**3.** The Khmers abandoned Angkor in the …
a) 14th century b) 13th century c) 12th century d) 11th century

**4.** Angkor Wat is the most beautiful temple because of all of the following, except:
a) carvings b) tall buildings c) architecture d) apsaras

**5.** The Khmer civilization was highly developed as shown by its …
a) temples b) sculptures c) a and b d) none of these

## 8 ONE MORE TIME

**Directions:**

# Trivia

**Make groups of four. One student is a Leader. The Leader opens the book, chooses 3 categories and asks the question from the chart below. The Group Members answer the questions. If the answer is correct, s/he gets a point. Take turns asking questions.**

**STRUCTURE:** (fast) ⇨ **a human** / an elephant

**Leader:** Which is **faster**, **a human** or **an elephant**?
**Member:** I think **an elephant** is **faster** than **a human**.
**Leader:** You're wrong. **A human** is **faster** than **an elephant**.

| HOT | TALL | EXPENSIVE | OLD | LUXURIOUS |
|---|---|---|---|---|
| **Cairo**<br>Tel Aviv | **Mount Everest**<br>K-2 | **Tokyo**<br>New York | Helicopter<br>**Airplane** | Caesars Palace Hotel<br>**Barj Al Arab Hotel** |
| **OLD** | **WET** | **QUIET** | **TALL** | **CHEAP** |
| **The Pyramids**<br>Angkor Wat | Manila<br>**Singapore** | **Resort**<br>City Hotel | **Taipei 101**<br>Petronas Towers | **A ticket to Daegu**<br>A ticket to Jeju-do |
| **BIG** | **FAMOUS** | **LONG** | **LARGE** | **HOT** |
| **China**<br>U.S.A | India<br>**France** | The Amazon River<br>**The Nile River** | **Pacific Ocean**<br>Atlantic Ocean | Bangkok<br>**Nairobi** |
| **DEEP** | **SMALL** | **DANGEROUS** | **LONG** | **SMALL** |
| Tonga Trench<br>**Mariana Trench** | **The Vatican**<br>Monaco | An airplane<br>**A car** | **The Danube**<br>Thames River | **The Seychelles**<br>Sudan |
| **BIG** | **LARGE** | **COLD** | **SHORT** | **WARM** |
| **Sahara Desert**<br>Gobi Desert | **Caspian Sea**<br>Lake Huron | **Montreal**<br>Berlin | **63 Building**<br>Empire State Bldg. | July in Iceland<br>**Jan. in Hong Kong** |

**SCORE CARD**

| NAME | | | | |
|---|---|---|---|---|
| SCORE | | | | |

# Chapter 5

## *Lost In New York!*

## ❶ KEY VOCABULARY

| | | | |
|---|---|---|---|
| Traffic Light | Rotary | Across from | To the left/right of |
| Intersection | Overpass | Corner | In the middle of |
| Zebra Crossing | Underpass | Next to | Behind |
| Opposite | Bridge | In front of | Over |
| Between | Railroad Tracks | Beside | Under |
| Around | Tunnel | At the back of | Past … |

## ❷ WARM-UP

➢ **Match the pictures with the correct sentences. Write the place in the white box.**

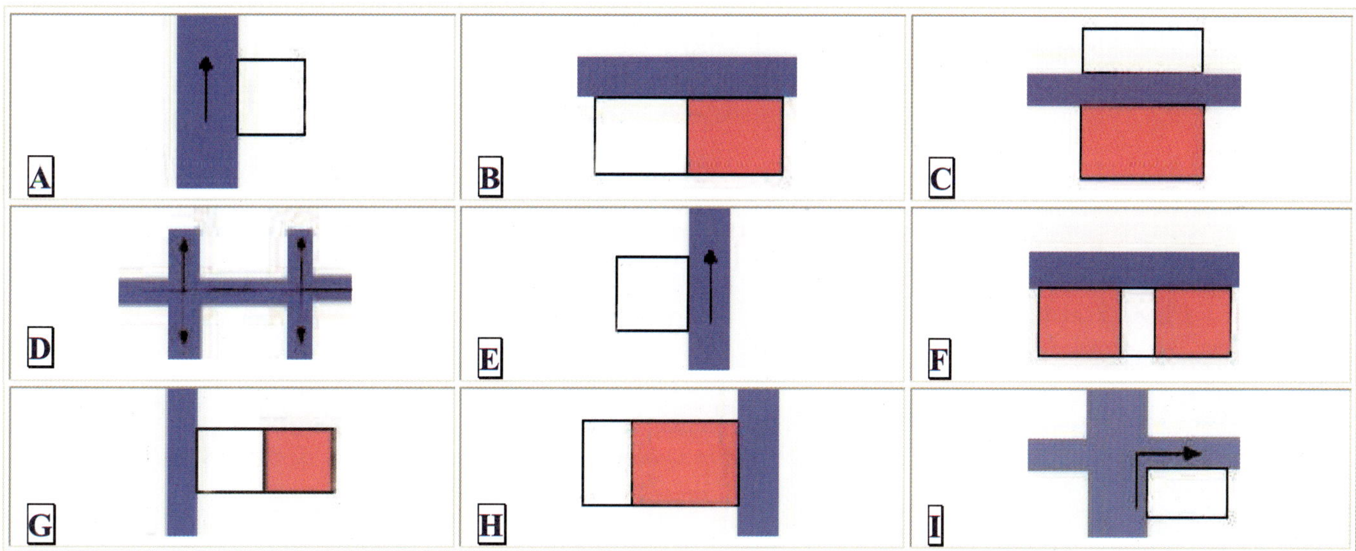


**1. The car rental is on the corner of $3^{rd}$ Avenue.**
**2. The health club is on your left.**
**3. The ballroom is next to the gift shop.**
**4. The bakery is on your right.**
**5. The hotel is between the travel agency and the coffee shop.**
**6. The beauty shop is opposite the bank.**
**7. The restaurant is behind the business center.**
**8. The intersection of $3^{rd}$ and $4^{th}$ street.**
**9. The florist is in front of the souvenir shop.**

## ❸ LANGUAGE STRUCTURE

| | |
|---|---|
| Go straight one (two, three, etc…) block(s). | It's the 1st (2nd, 3rd, etc..) building on your right/left |
| Turn right/left | It's between the ……….and the ………. |
| Turn right/left at the ……… | It's across from the …….. |
| Take the 1st (2nd, 3rd, etc…) right/left | Go past the ………. |
| Go around the rotary | It's on/around the corner |
| Go over the overpass | It's across the street |

| ASKING FOR DIRECTIONS | GIVING DIRECTIONS |
|---|---|
| **How do I get to** the coffee shop? | Go straight ______ (number) block(s) on______ (name of street).<br>Turn right/left onto _________ (name of street).<br>It's __________. |
| **Where is** the bank? | It's __________ (near/around the corner from/across from/beside/behind/in front of) the _________ (name of place). |
| **Is there** a beauty shop near here? | Yes, there is. It's _________ (across the street/in the shopping mall on first street/over there).<br>No, there isn't one around here. |
| Excuse me. I'm looking for a health club.<br>**Is there one** near here? | Yes, there's one over there.<br>No, there isn't any near here. |

➢ **Look at the map below and fill in the blanks.**

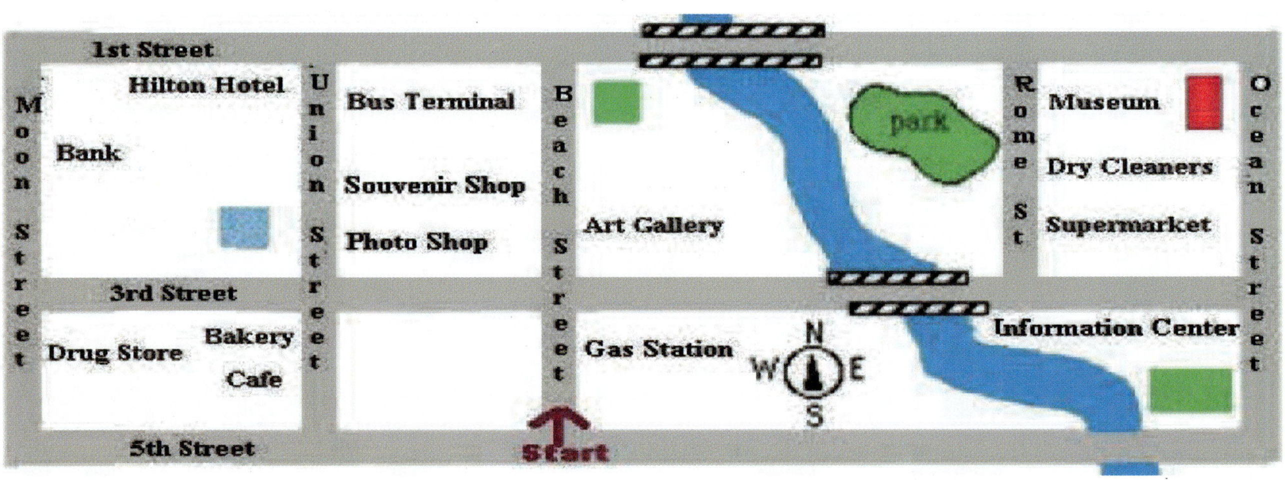


1. Go _______ 1 block on Beach Street. Turn right onto 3rd Street and go ___________ the railroad tracks. It's on your right. You're at the ___________________.
2. Go 2 blocks West on 5th Street. Turn right at the _________ and go _______ the bank. It's on your right. You'll reach the ____________________.
3. Go east on 5th Street ________ the overpass. Turn left onto ______, take the 1st left, and go straight 1 block. Turn on Rome Street. It's _________ the supermarket and the museum. You're at the ___________________.
4. Go ________ block West on 5th Street. Turn right on Union Street. Keep going until you've reached the souvenir shop. It's ______ from the Hilton Hotel. You've reached the ______.

## ❹ CONVERSATION

➢ **Practice the following dialogue with a partner.**

**Kyung Ah:** Excuse me, I'm lost. **How do I get to** the Plaza Hotel? ①
**Henry:** Go straight and take the **4th left**. ❶
**Kyung Ah:** The **1st left**? ②
**Henry:** No. The **4th left … 1st, 2nd, 3rd, 4th**. ❷
**Kyung Ah:** I see … the **4th left**. ③
**Henry:** That's correct. Then go straight 3 blocks. You'll get to **50th** Street. ❸
**Kyung Ah:** Did you say **15th** Street? ④
**Henry:** No! No! **Not 15th Street … 49th, 50th**. ❹
**Kyung Ah:** Oh, okay. **50th** Street. ⑤
**Henry:** Walk 2 blocks East until you reach the light …
**Kyung Ah:** Turn right?
**Henry:** You know what, **just follow me**! ❺
**Kyung Ah:** Oh … you're so kind.

## SUBSTITUTION DRILL

➢ **Substitute with the words or phrases below:**

| Kyung Ah | Henry |
|---|---|
| ① Where is<br>Which way is it to<br>Do you know the way to | ❶ 1st left<br>4th right<br>1st right |
| ② 4th left<br>1st right<br>4th right | ❷ 1st left …<br>4th right …1st, 2nd, 3rd, 4th.<br>1st right. |
| ③ 1st left<br>4th right<br>1st right | ❸ 70th<br>40th<br>60th |
| ④ 17th<br>14th<br>16th | ❹ Not 17th Street … 69th, 70th<br>Not 14th Street … 39th, 40th<br>Not 16th Street … 59th, 60th |
| ⑤ 70th<br>40th<br>60th | ❺ I'll take you there!<br>come with me!<br>I'll show you the way! |

## ❺ CHALLENGE YOURSELF

**Part One:** **Read the directions and label the map below.**

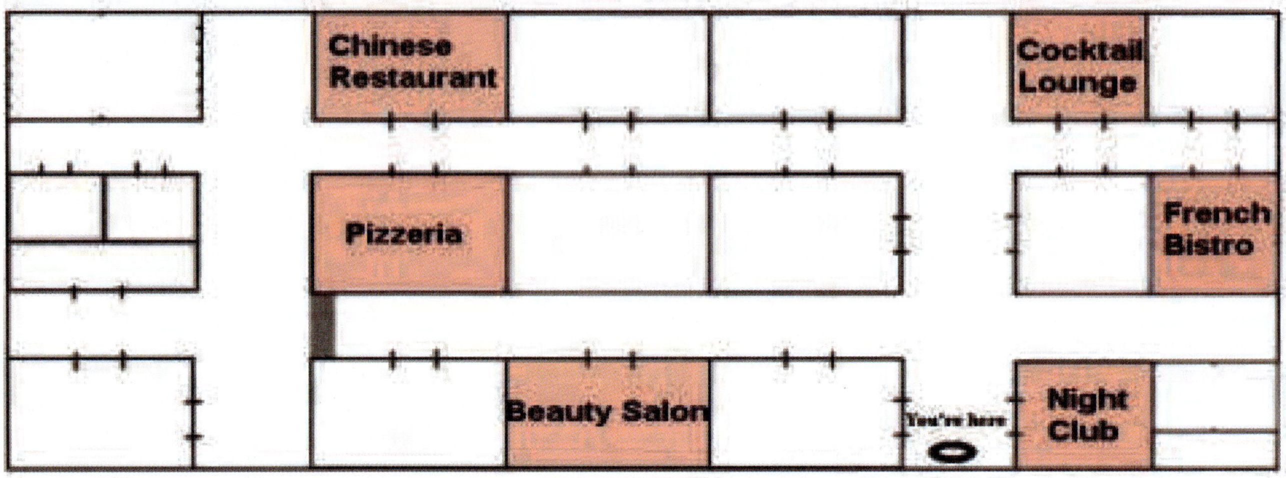


**Directions:**

**A.** Take the 1st left and go straight. The **business center** is to the left of the beauty salon.

**B.** Take the 2nd left. Go past the Chinese Restaurant. The **ballroom** is in front of you, on your right.

**C.** Take the 1st right. The **escalators** are on your right.

**D.** Take the 2nd left. The **florist** is the 2nd store on your left.

**E.** Take the 2nd right. The **coffee shop** is on your left, opposite the French Bistro.

**F.** Take the 2nd left. Turn left at the Chinese Restaurant. Go past the pizzeria.
The **health club** is on your right.

**Part Two:** **Label the above map with the given places below. Then give directions to your partner. Take turns describing the location of a place. Can your partner guess which place you're describing?**

- **Kiosk**
- **Health Club**
- **Ladies' Room**
- **Deli**

## ❻-1 PAIR WORK

**STUDENT A**

| QUESTIONS | ANSWERS |
|---|---|
| Excuse me. How do I get to the gym? | Go straight 2 block(s) on Wood Drive. Turn left onto 12th Street. It's the 3rd building on your right. |
| Thank you. | You're welcome. |

**Part One:** Look at the map and write the directions to the places.

1. Bakery: ______________________
2. Post office: ______________________
3. 7-11: ______________________
4. Café: ______________________
5. Mall: ______________________
6. Travel Agency: ______________________

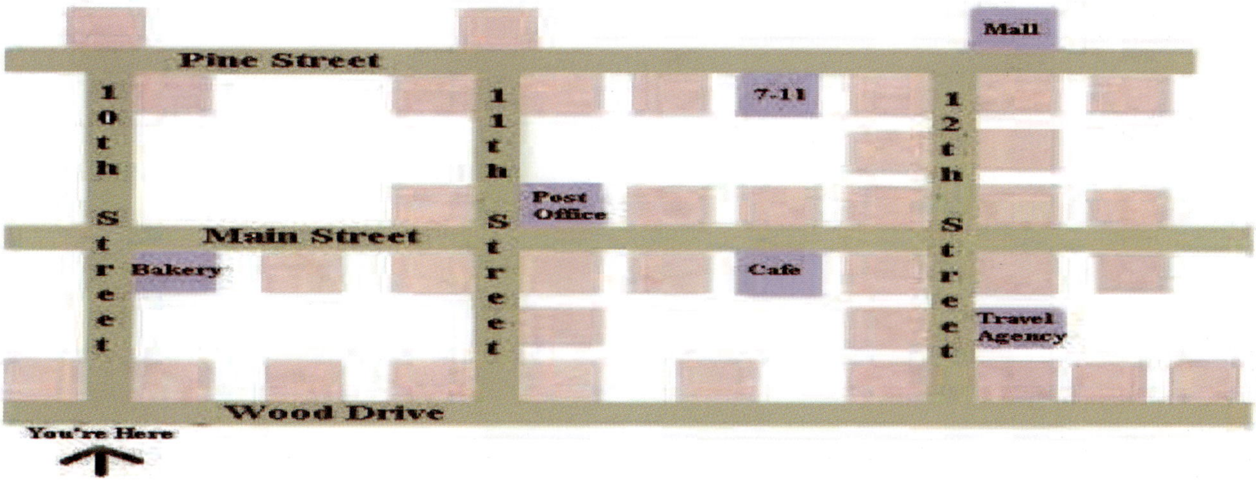


**Part Two:** Ask STUDENT B for directions to the following places and label the map.

- ❒ 1. Bus Stop
- ❒ 2. Florist
- ❒ 3. ATM
- ❒ 4. Deli
- ❒ 5. W Hotel
- ❒ 6. Taxi Stand

## ❻-2 PAIR WORK

**STUDENT B**

| QUESTIONS | ANSWERS |
|---|---|
| Excuse me. How do I get to the gym? | Go straight 2 block(s) on Wood Drive. Turn left onto 12th Street. It's the 3rd building on your right. |
| Thank you. | You're welcome. |

**Part One:** Look at the map and write the directions to the places.

1. Bus Stop: ______________________________
2. Florist: ______________________________
3. ATM: ______________________________
4. Deli: ______________________________
5. W Hotel: ______________________________
6. Taxi Stand: ______________________________

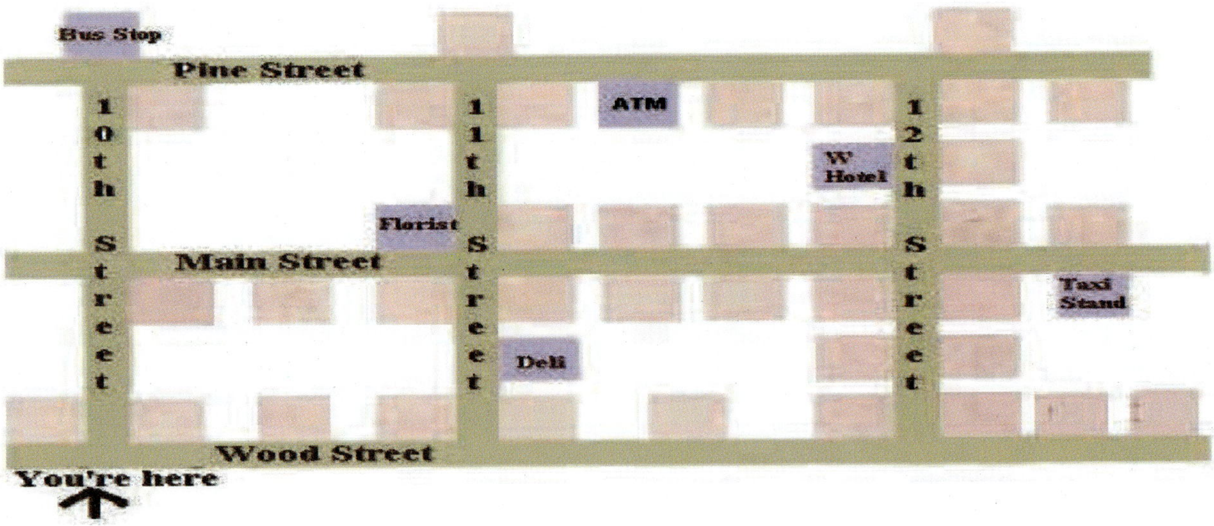


**Part Two:** Ask STUDENT A for directions to the following places and label the map.

- ❒ 1. Bakery
- ❒ 2. Post Office
- ❒ 3. 7-11
- ❒ 4. Café
- ❒ 5. Mall
- ❒ 6. Travel Agency

## 7 READING

# Why Is New York City Called "The Big Apple"?

1 Why is New York City called the Big Apple? This is the most frequently asked question by visitors to New York City. In popular folklore, the name is usually traced to early jazz musicians or sports figures. But in reality it dates back to the early nineteenth century.

2 In the early years of the nineteenth century, Europeans began arriving in New York in great numbers." Arriving here without money or friends, many of these were forced to survive, as one person put it, "by their wits or worse."

3 Evelyn Claudine de Saint-Évremond arrived in New York in 1803. Evelyn was very attractive, beautiful, vivacious, and well-educated. She established a salon with the help of friends. The salon was an elegantly furnished bordello -- in a big house that still stands at 142 Bond Street.

4 Evelyn's establishment was a success, and for several decades maintained, a good reputation as the city's best "temple of love," a place not only for lovemaking, but also for elegant dinners, high-stakes gambling, and good conversation. The girls, many of them arrivals from Paris or London, were noted for their beauty.

5 New Yorkers gave Evelyn the nickname of "Eve" Evelyn found this biblical name highly amusing, and thereafter referred to the ladies that she employed as "my irresistible apples." The young men-about-town soon got into the habit of referring to their adventures as "having a taste of Eve's Apples." Ever since then New York has been known as the Big Apple.

## COMPREHENSION

◆ **Match the words in Column A and Column B to make sentences.**

| ANSWERS | A | B |
|---|---|---|
| ________ | **1.** Evelyn opened up | **a.** had a good reputation. |
| ________ | **2.** The "temple of love" employed | **b.** New York City. |
| ________ | **3.** New Yorkers gave Evelyn | **c.** a salon. |
| ________ | **4.** The Nickname of Eve | **d.** beautiful European girls. |
| ________ | **5.** Eve's business | **e.** the nickname Eve. |
| ________ | **6.** The Big Apple refers to | **f.** came from the bible. |

## 8 ONE MORE TIME

# Hide and Seek

◆ **SCENARIO:**

**STUDENT A is hiding somewhere in the airport. The other two students will listen to the directions and will try to find where Student A is.**

☑ **Work in groups of three. Student A gives directions. Students B/C follow the directions and will try to guess where student A is. Take turns being student A.**

**STRUCTURE:**

| | |
|---|---|
| **Student A:** | Are you ready? |
| **Students B/C:** | Yes, we are. |
| **Student A:** | Listen to my directions and try to find me. |
| **Students B/C:** | Okay. We're listening. |
| **Student A:** | **Turn right**. Go **past** the **Business Class Lounge** and turn **left** at the **Currency Exchanger**. I'm on your **left**. Where am I? |
| **Student B:** | Oh, I know … you're at the **Duty Free Shop**! |
| **Student A:** | Yes, I am. But you must look **higher**. |
| **Student C:** | Are you **on top of** the **Duty Free Shop**? |
| **Student A:** | Yes, I am. |

## AIRPORT CHECK-IN

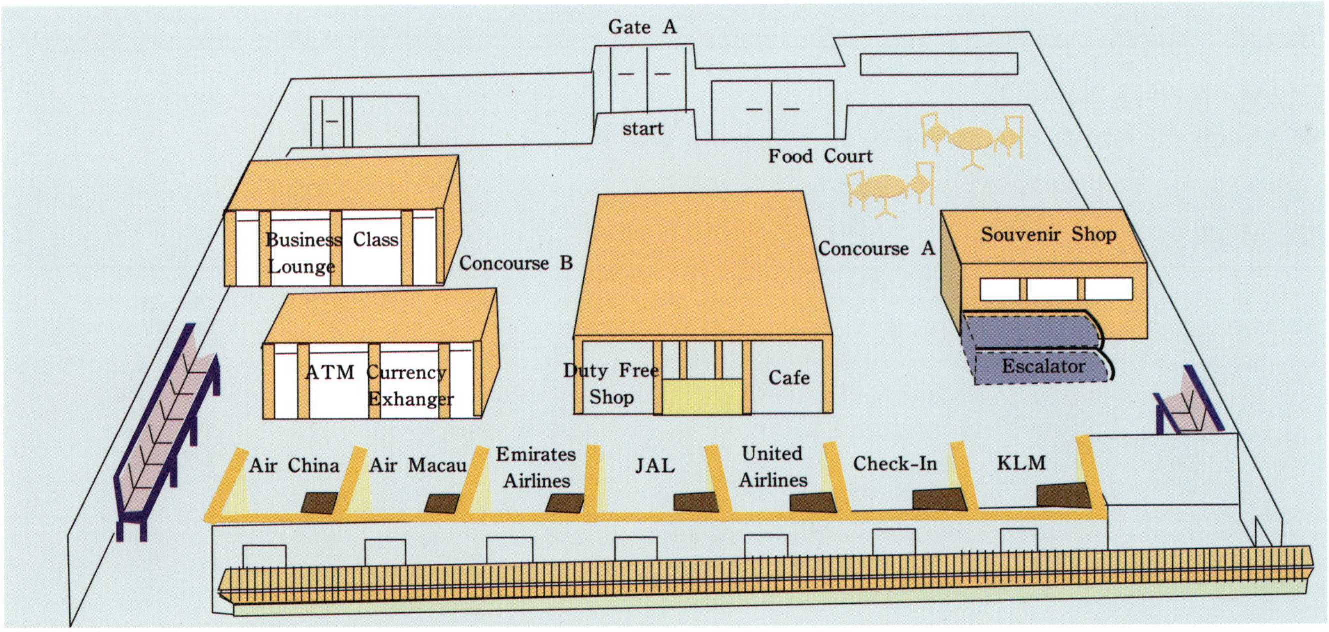

# Chapter 6

## *A Honeymoon Suite With A View, Please.*

## ❶ KEY VOCABULARY

| | | | |
|---|---|---|---|
| Voucher | Tax | Reservation | Surname |
| Traveler's Check | Service Charge | Area Code | Special Request |
| Supplemental Charge | Twin | Contact Number | Prefer |
| Expiration Date | Net | Deluxe Room | Confirm |
| Serviced Apartments | Rate/Tariff | Arrival Date | Double Room |
| Boutique Hotel | Adjoining Room | Departure Date | Vacancy |

## ❷ WARM-UP

➤ **Make groups of three. Ask and answer the questions below.**

TRA-36807-1
Name:
Peter Jones
Hotel:
Mercure Hevelius Gdansk (tel. 058/3210022, fax. 058/3210020)
ul. Heweliusza 22, Gdansk
Room type:
2 bed(s) 2 person(s)
Number of rooms: 1
Number of guests per room: 2
Arrival date: 2004-07-28
Departure date: 2004-08-01

**What do you think this is?**
I think this is a ____________________.
**When is the check-in date?**
It's ____________________.
**When is the check-out date?**
It's ____________________.
**How many guests will be staying?**
There will be ________________.
**What type of room does Mr. Jones want?**
He wants a ____________________.

**What is this?** This is a __________.
**How much is it worth?**
It's worth $ ______________.

**What kind of credit card is this?** It's a ________________.
**What is the expiration date?** It's ____________________.
**What is the cardholder's surname?** His surname is ________.

Oakwood

**What type of hotel is Oakwood?**
It's a ________________.
**Is there an Oakwood hotel in your country?** Yes, there is.
It's in ____________. No, there isn't.

HYATT

**Park Hyatt Milan**
**Daily Rate: 426 Euros ++**

**What does ++ stand for?** I think it means ____________.
**What is the tariff?** It's ____________________.
**Where is Milan?** It's in ____________________.

## ❸ LANGUAGE STRUCTURE

| RESERVATION CLERK | GUEST |
|---|---|
| What's your name? | My name is ________________. |
| How do you spell your family name? | It's ________________. |
| When will you arrive, sir/madam? | I'll arrive on ______________ (date). |
| How many nights will you be staying with us? | I'll be staying for _______ night(s). |
| What type of room do you prefer? | I prefer a _____________ room. |
| How many people are there in your family? | There are __________ people. |
| What is your contact number? | My contact number is __________. |
| How would you like to pay, sir/madam? | I'll pay by ______________. |
| May I have your credit card number and the expiration date, please? | The card number is ___________, and the expiration date is _______________. |

**Part One:** **Fill out the reservation form. Ask your partner the above questions and complete his/her card.**

| YOURSELF | YOUR PARTNER |
|---|---|
| Guest Name: ____________________________ | Guest Name: ____________________________ |
| Arrival Date: ____________________________ | Arrival Date: ____________________________ |
| Departure Date: __________________________ | Departure Date: __________________________ |
| Room Type: _____________________________ | Room Type: _____________________________ |
| No. of Persons: __________________________ | No. of Persons: __________________________ |
| Method of Payment:____________ (Credit Card) | Method of Payment:____________ (Credit Card) |
| ❒ Card Number: _____________________ | ❒ Card Number: _____________________ |
| ❒ Expiration Date: _____/_____/ (MM/YY) | ❒ Expiration Date: _____/_____/ (MM/YY) |
| Contact Number: __________________________ | Contact Number: __________________________ |

**Part Two:** **Work with a partner and answer the questions below.**

1. Name as many types of credit cards as you can: ______________________________
2. How many ways can guests pay for a hotel room? ______________________________
3. Think of as many hotel rooms as you can: ______________________________
4. List as many area codes in your country as you can: ______________________________
5. List as many hotel chains as you can: ______________________________
6. Name as many 5 star hotels in your country as you can: ______________________________
7. What are some special requests guests can make? ______________________________
8. Come up with as many discounted hotel websites as you can: ______________________________
9. Think of as many world currencies as you can: ______________________________
10. Name as many hotel facilities as you can: ______________________________

**Part Three:** **Close your textbook. Listen to your teacher and answer the questions.**

## ❹ CONVERSATION

➤ **Practice the following dialogue with a partner.**

**Tracy:** Good morning. Westin Sydney. Tracy speaking…
**Daniel:** Is this the Westin Sydney?
**Tracy:** Yes, it is. **May I help you**? ①
**Daniel:** Certainly. I'd like to **reserve** the honeymoon suite with a view, please! ❶
**Tracy:** When will you **arrive**, sir? ②
**Daniel:** I'll be **arriving** on June 12th. ❷
**Tracy:** When will **you be leaving**? ③
**Daniel:** On the 17th of June.
**Tracy:** Could I have your last name, please?
**Daniel:** It's Fisher.
**Tracy:** How would you like to pay, Mr. Fisher?
**Daniel:** I'll pay by **Amex**. ❸
**Tracy:** May I have your card number and the expiration date?
**Daniel:** 3672 965000 57543 and the expiration date is 11/08.
**Tracy:** **What's your contact number**, sir? ④
**Daniel:** **I can be reached at** 1-613-828-5543. ❹
**Tracy:** Thank you, Mr. Fisher. We look forward to seeing you on June 12th.

## SUBSTITUTION DRILL

➤ **Substitute with the words or phrases below:**

| Tracy | Daniel |
|---|---|
| ① What can I do for you<br>How can I help you<br>How can I assist you | ❶ book<br>make a reservation for<br>arrange |
| ② check-in<br>come here<br>be staying with us | ❷ checking-in<br>coming here<br>staying at your hotel |
| ③ you be checking-out<br>you be departing<br>your departure date be | ❸ Visa<br>MasterCard<br>Diners Club |
| ④ Where can you be reached<br>Do you have a contact number<br>How can we contact you | ❹ My contact number is<br>The phone number is<br>You can reach me at |

## ❺ CHALLENGE YOURSELF

◆ You are a RESERVATION CLERK. Use the chart below to confirm Mr. Fisher's reservation. Refer to the previous dialogue.

**Confirmation:**

**G. You're booked in a ____________________ from __________ to __________.**
**H. The room rate is $ _______ plus _____%________, and _______% _________.**
**I. Your contact number is ______________________.**

Room Availability: ■ Available ■ Booked

Westin Sydney

JUNE

| Sun | Mon | Tues | Wed | Thurs | Fri | Sat |
|---|---|---|---|---|---|---|
| (Available) | 1 (Booked) | 2 (Booked) | 3 (Available) | 4 (Available) | 5 (Available) | 6 (Available) |
| 7 (Available) | 8 (Booked) | 9 (Available) | 10 (Booked) | 11 (Available) | 12 (Available) | 13 (Available) |
| 14 (Available) | 15 (Available) | 16 (Available) | 17 (Booked) | 18 (Booked) | 19 (Available) | 20 (Booked) |
| 21 (Booked) | 22 (Available) | 23 (Available) | 24 (Available) | 25 (Booked) | 26 (Booked) | 27 (Booked) |
| 28 (Available) | 29 (Available) | 30 (Available) | | | | |

**Rates:** **Single: AU$295** **Double Deluxe: AU$365** **Twin: AU$345** **Junior Suite: AU$995**
**Honeymoon Suite: AU$875** **•All rates are subject to 10% tax and 10% service charge.**

◆

**STRUCTURE:**

**G:** Do you have a **double deluxe** room available on **June 1st**?
**R:** I'm sorry, but we're booked solid.
**G:** When will a room become available?
**R:** We have one room free on **June 3rd**.
**G:** Okay. How much is it?
**R:** It's **$140** plus tax and service charge.
**G:** That's great. I'll take it.

---

**G: Guest R: Reservation Clerk**

**① You are a GUEST. Use the structure on the left. You want to book the following rooms:**

- ❑ Junior Suite (June 16th)
- ❑ Single (June 23rd )

**② Now You are a RESERVATION CLERK. Answer the Guest's questions.**

**① You are a RESERVATION CLERK. Use the structure on the left to answer the Guest's questions.**

**② Now you are a GUEST. You want to book the following rooms:**

- ❑ Honeymoon Suite (June 12th)
- ❑ Twin (June 13th )

## 6-1 PAIR WORK

**STUDENT A**

| RESERVATION CLERK | GUEST |
|---|---|
| **Intercontinental Hotel.** How may I help you? | Yes, I'd like to make a reservation. |
| When will you arrive, **sir**? | I'll check-in on **February 19th**. |
| When will you check-out? | I'll check-out on **February 21st**. |
| What kind of room would you like? | I prefer a **double**. |
| How many people are there in your party? | There will be **2**. |
| May I have your name? | My name is **Joshua Santos**. |
| How do you spell your family name? | It's **S-A-N-T-O-S**. |
| Where can you be reached? | My contact number is **1-201-876-2331**. |
| How would you like to pay, **Mr. Santos**? | I'd like to pay by **Amex**. |
| May I have the card number and expiration date, please? | My card number is **35782-810031-46291** and the expiration date is **09/10**. |
| You're confirmed from **Feb. 19th** to **Feb. 21st** in a **double**. The room rate is **$315** + **5** % tax and **10** % service charge. You can be contacted at **1-201-876-2331**. Is that correct? | Yes, it is. |
| Is there anything else, **Mr. Santos**? | Yes, I'd like a **room with a good view**. |
| Certainly, **Mr. Santos**. Enjoy your day! | You're welcome. Bye! |

**Part One:** You are a RESERVATION CLERK. Take the reservation and fill out the form.

Reservation (MANDARIN ORIENTAL THE HOTEL GROUP) Form

| | | | |
|---|---|---|---|
| **Guest Name:** | ________ | **Departure Date:** | ________ |
| **Arrival Date:** | ________ | **Room Rate:** | **$535** |
| **Room Type:** | ________ | **Contact Number:** | ________ |
| **Number of Guests:** | ________ | **Card Number:** | ________ |
| **Payment:** | ________ | **Expiration Date:** | ____/____ (MM/YY) |
| **Special Request:** | ________ | | |

*All rates subject to 5% tax and 10% service charge.

**Part Two:** You are a GUEST. Use the information below to make a reservation.

| | |
|---|---|
| **Name:** Carol Schwartz | **Departure Date:** September 23rd |
| **Arrival:** September 18th | **Number of Guests:** 2 adults and a baby |
| **Room:** Double | **Card Number:** 5300 7566 1330 7017 6012 |
| **Payment:** Master Card | **Expiration Date:** 11/08 |
| **Phone No:** 1-212-785-8018 | |
| **Special Request:** baby crib in the room | |

## 6-2 PAIR WORK

**STUDENT B**

| RESERVATION CLERK | GUEST |
|---|---|
| **Intercontinental Hotel**. How may I help you? | Yes, I'd like to make a reservation. |
| When will you arrive, **sir**? | I'll check-in on **February 19th**. |
| When will you check-out? | I'll check-out on **February 21st**. |
| What kind of room would you like? | I prefer a **double**. |
| How many people are there in your party? | There will be **2**. |
| May I have your name? | My name is **Joshua Santos**. |
| How do you spell your family name? | It's **S-A-N-T-O-S**. |
| Where can you be reached? | My contact number is **1-201-876-2331**. |
| How would you like to pay, **Mr. Santos**? | I'd like to pay by **Amex**. |
| May I have the card number and expiration date, please? | My card number is **35782-810031-46291** and the expiration date is **09/10**. |
| You're confirmed from **Feb. 19th** to **Feb. 21st** in a **double**. The room rate is **$315** + **5** % tax and **10** % service charge. You can be contacted at **1-201-876-2331**. Is that correct? | Yes, it is. |
| Is there anything else, **Mr. Santos**? | Yes, I'd like a **room with a good view**. |
| Certainly, **Mr. Santos**. Enjoy your day! | You're welcome. Bye! |

**Part One:** You are a GUEST. Use the information below to make a reservation.

**Name:** David Willis
**Arrival:** March 30th
**Room:** Suite
**Payment:** Amex
**Phone No:** 1-203-515-2012
**Special Request:** bottle of champagne in my suite
**Departure Date:** April 1st
**Number of Guests:** myself
**Card Number:** 3654 842000 49835
**Expiration Date:** 10/09

**Part Two:** You are a RESERVATION CLERK. Take the reservation and fill out the form.

Raffles Hotels & Resorts
**Reservation Form**

**Guest Name:** ____________
**Arrival Date:** ____________
**Room Type:** ____________
**Number of Guests:** ____________
**Payment:** ____________
**Special Request:** ____________
**Departure Date:** ____________
**Room Rate:** $160
**Contact Number:** ____________
**Card Number:** ____________
**Expiration Date:** ______/______ (MM/YY)

*All rates subject to 10% tax and 5% service charge.

## 7 READING

### The Ice Hotel

1 Imagine staying at a hotel built entirely out of ice. The thought of someone constructing an entire hotel out of ice, rent rooms and repeat the process each year seems unbelievable but it does exist. These ice hotels have become the trendiest way to spend a winter vacation.

2 The first Ice Hotel was built in 1989 in a village called Jukkasjärvi in northern Lapland, Sweden. Construction begins each year in October, and the hotel is open for guests from December through April (weather permitting). By summer the hotel has melted and the whole process of re- building begins again in October.

3 Ice hotels are built, naturally, entirely out of frozen water in the form of ice blocks and hard-packed snow. The guest rooms contain beds made of a block of ice and topped with a foam mattress. You sleep in sleeping bags covered with animal skins. Although the air temperature in the room is below freezing, your body remains warm. If nature calls in the middle of the night, you can go to the bathroom in the adjoining heated building.

4 Although the design changes from year to year, Sweden's Ice Hotel includes an ice bar for vodka-based drinks (beer would freeze); even the glasses and plates are made of ice. There's also an ice chapel for "white" weddings, an ice cinema, an ice sauna and ice art galleries, Most guests stay only one night in an ice room; ordinary heated hotel rooms are available nearby for longer stays. Even so, the hotel has a waiting list several years long.

## COMPREHENSION

◆ **Circle the correct answer.**

**1.** How frequent do they build the Ice Hotel?
a) annually b) bi annually c) every 2 years d) 3 times per year

**2.** How many months in a year is the Ice Hotel open?
a) 4 months b) 5 months c) 6 months d) 7 months

**3.** All of the following can be found in the guest room, except:
a) bed b) sleeping bags c) bathroom d) mattress

**4.** Amenities found in this hotel are all of the following, except:
a) sauna b) galleries c) beer bar d) cinema

**5.** How many nights do guests usually stay?
a) 2 nights b) one week c) 3 nights d) overnight

## 8 ONE MORE TIME

# Outburst

☑ Make groups of four. Group A chooses a category. Group B has one minute to yell out as many answers that fit into the category as possible. Group A will check the corresponding boxes and count to see how many points Group B gets. Take turn choosing a category. Each category can only be used once. Have Fun!

| HOTEL CHAINS | | TYPES OF ROOM | |
|---|---|---|---|
| ❒Hilton Hotel | ❒Westin Hotel | ❒Single | ❒Twin |
| ❒Sheraton Hotel | ❒Intercontinental Hotel | ❒Family Room | ❒Superior |
| ❒Marriot Hotel | ❒Holiday Inn | ❒Double | ❒Executive |
| ❒Traders Hotel | ❒Shangri-La | ❒Deluxe Room | ❒Honeymoon Suite |
| ❒Ritz Carton | ❒Novotel | ❒Junior Suite | ❒Presidential Suite |

| HOTEL FACILITIES | | JOBS IN HOTEL | |
|---|---|---|---|
| ❒Swimming Pool | ❒Tennis Court | ❒Bell Boy | ❒Chauffeur |
| ❒Fitness Center | ❒Night Club | ❒Housekeeper | ❒Concierge |
| ❒Business Center | ❒Conference Room | ❒Lifeguard | ❒Waiter |
| ❒Restaurant | ❒In-room Safe | ❒Chef | ❒Casino Dealer |
| ❒Room Service | ❒Dry Cleaning Service | ❒Receptionist | ❒Maitre d' |

| METHOD OF PAYMENT | | SPECIAL REQUESTS | |
|---|---|---|---|
| ❒Cash | ❒Master Card | ❒Champagne in Room | ❒Sea View / Ocean View |
| ❒Voucher | ❒Amex | ❒Airport Pick-Up | ❒Newspaper |
| ❒T.C | ❒Diners Club | ❒Baby Crib in Room | ❒Airport Drop-Off |
| ❒JCB Card | ❒Carte Blanc | ❒Wake-Up Call | ❒Handicap Parking |
| ❒Visa | ❒Euro card | ❒Late Check-In | ❒Boxed Breakfast |

| ASIAN COUNTRIES | | EUROPEAN CAPITALS | |
|---|---|---|---|
| ❒The Philippines | ❒Mongolia | ❒Budapest | ❒Rome |
| ❒Thailand | ❒India | ❒Berlin | ❒Prague |
| ❒Singapore | ❒Vietnam | ❒Vienna | ❒Athens |
| ❒Myanmar | ❒Cambodia | ❒Copenhagen | ❒Bern |
| ❒Malaysia | ❒Indonesia | ❒Paris | ❒London |

| WORLD CURRENCIES | | AIRLINES | |
|---|---|---|---|
| ❒Australian Dollar | ❒Baht | ❒United Airlines | ❒Thai International |
| ❒Euro | ❒Rupees | ❒Air Canada | ❒British Airways |
| ❒Pound | ❒Francs | ❒Lufthansa | ❒Aeroflot |
| ❒Yen | ❒Rand | ❒Singapore Airlines | ❒Emirates |
| ❒Peso | ❒Renminbi Yuan | ❒Cathay Pacific | ❒China Airlines |

# Chapter 7

## *Be Our Guest!*

## ❶ KEY VOCABULARY

| | | | |
|---|---|---|---|
| Walk-in | Wake-up Call | Elevator | Occupation |
| Registration Card/Form | Signature/Sign | View | Zip Code/Postal Code |
| Imprint/Swipe | Luggage/Bag | Emergency Contact | Escalator |
| Nationality | Ground Floor | Overnight | Front Desk |
| Fill-in/Fill-out | Leaflet/Pamphlet | Underground Parking | Register |
| Key Card | Next Destination | Complimentary | Passport Number |

## ❷ WARM-UP

➢ **Work with a partner. Fill in the blank boxes. The first one is already done for you.**

### Guest Registration Card

**Full Name:** Sandra Bullock

________: 85 Rodeo Drive
Beverly Hills, California
90210 U.S.A

________: July 1st
________: July 4th
________: 3 nights
________: 2 people
________: Diners Club

________: Junior Suite
________: Suite 23
________: $400++

**Overseas Visitors**

________: American
________: 111117994
________: Bangkok

________: *Sandra Bullock*

**Note: All guests should check-out before 1 p.m.**

## 3 LANGUAGE STRUCTURE

| FRONT DESK | GUEST |
|---|---|
| May I have your passport, please? | Here it is. |
| Could you fill out this registration form, please? | Of course. Here you are. |
| How will you be paying sir/madam? | JCB Card. |
| Is it okay if I take an imprint of your card? | Sure. Go ahead! |
| Would you like any help with your bags? | Yes, I need a bell boy to bring my bags to the room. |

➤ **Use the information in the box to complete the dialogue.**

**FRONT DESK RECEPTIONIST**

Thank-you. You're in room 2012 which is on the 20th floor.
Please fill out this registration card.
May I swipe your card, please?
It's served from 6:30 – 10:00 in the coffee shop. Enjoy your stay with us!
Welcome to Manila Peninsula. How may I assist you?
Yes, it does. Can I have a bellman bring the bags to your room?
You have a reservation for a double room for 1 night. Is that correct?
How will you be paying Mr. Brown?
May I have your passport, please?

### DIALOGUE

**Front Desk:** ______________________________.
**Mr. Brown:** I have a reservation. My name is Sean Brown.
**Front Desk:** ______________________________.
**Mr. Brown:** Yes, it is.
**Front Desk:** ______________________________.
**Mr. Brown:** Here you are.
**Front Desk:** ______________________________.
**Mr. Brown:** Of course.
**Front Desk:** ______________________________.
**Mr. Brown:** Euro Card.
**Front Desk:** ______________________________.
**Mr. Brown:** Sure, you can.
**Front Desk:** ______________________________.
**Mr. Brown:** Great! Does the room have a good view?
**Front Desk:** ______________________________.
**Mr. Brown:** Yes. What time is breakfast served?
**Front Desk:** ______________________________.
**Mr. Brown:** I will. Thank-you.

## ④ CONVERSATION

➤ **Practice the following dialogue with a partner.**

**Krista:** Welcome to Westin Sydney Hotel. How may I help you?
**Daniel:** Yes, my name is Daniel Fisher. **May I talk to Tracy**? ❶
**Krista:** I'm afraid **it's her day off today**. Is there anything I can do for you Mr. Fisher?①
**Daniel:** I've made a reservation over the phone and **requested** an airport pick-up. ❷
**Krista:** Please wait a moment…I'm sorry Mr. Fisher. But **your request is not in our computer**.②
**Daniel:** Fine! **We had a long flight**. Could you just give us the key to our room? ❸
**Krista:** Please fill out this registration form. I'll have the bellboy **bring the bags** to your room?③
**Daniel:** All right. But we're **really tired**. Here you are. ❹
**Krista:** Let me **just confirm** if everything is correct. You'll be staying with us ④ until the 16th in the honeymoon suite…
**Daniel:** I can't believe this! We are supposed to **check-out** on the 17th. ❺
**Krista:** We **are terribly sorry**, Mr. Fisher. That's not a problem. But could I have your credit card so I can swipe it. And you'll be all set. ⑤
**Daniel:** You must be joking! Anyway, here it is.
**Krista:** Thank-you. I'm sure we can make it up to you.

## SUBSTITUTION DRILL

➤ **Substitute with the words or phrases below:**

| Daniel | Krista |
|---|---|
| ❶ May I speak to Tracy<br>Is Tracy here<br>Is Tracy available | ① she's not here today<br>she's on leave<br>she's no longer with us |
| ❷ asked for<br>arranged for<br>ordered | ② we don't have a record of it<br>we don't have it on file<br>I can't find it in our computer |
| ❸ It's been a stressful day<br>It's been a hectic day for us<br>The trip was very long | ③ show you to your room<br>carry the bags<br>take your luggage |
| ❹ exhausted<br>very sleepy<br>worn out | ④ check<br>verify<br>see |
| ❺ leave<br>depart<br>catch a flight | ⑤ apologize<br>regret this inconvenience<br>are so sorry |

## ❺ CHALLENGE YOURSELF

**Part One:** **Work with a partner. Unscramble the words using the given clues.**

| Hints: | Unscramble Words | Scrambled Words |
|---|---|---|
| **(A)** This means free. | ➔ ______________ | **miapomyctnrel** |
| **(B)** Chinese, Canadian and British are examples of this. | ➔ ______________ | **oaaltitniyn** |
| **(C)** You can see the ocean from your hotel room. | ➔ ______________ | **wiev** |
| **(D)**You can open your hotel room with this. | ➔ ______________ | **yke radc** |
| **(E)** Write one's name on a document is to do this. | ➔ ______________ | **ings** |
| **(F)** Another word for one night. | ➔ ______________ | **hgvnretio** |
| **(G)** Hilton, Sheraton and Hyatt are examples of these. | ➔ ______________ | **tolhe shanic** |
| **(H)** Before you go to your room, you must do this first. | ➔ ______________ | **sertgier** |
| **(I)** This is the person who takes your bags to your room. | ➔ ______________ | **lebobly** |
| **(J)** London, Toronto or Beijing might be examples of this. | ➔ ______________ | **xetn stindenatio** |
| **(K)** The receptionist takes this of your credit card. | ➔ ______________ | **pntriim** |
| **(L)** When you check-in you fill out this form. | ➔ ______________ | **risoginaertt** |
| **(M)** A booklet about the hotel facilities. | ➔ ______________ | **taplmpeh** |
| **(N)** Health club and beauty parlor are examples of these. | ➔ ______________ | **ialsifteci** |
| **(O)** You check-in here. | ➔ ______________ | **tfrno sedk** |

**Part Two:** **Find the above words in the puzzle. Circle the words.**

| | | | | | | | | | | | | | | |
|---|---|---|---|---|---|---|---|---|---|---|---|---|---|---|
| N | G | I | S | H | C | B | E | L | L | B | O | Y | D | T |
| W | E | Z | R | I | O | C | D | T | O | H | E | R | C | E |
| P | I | X | Q | H | M | N | A | G | Y | L | A | E | S | L |
| H | M | K | T | I | P | X | R | H | B | C | S | R | N | H |
| U | P | Q | L | D | L | O | K | E | Y | M | E | X | I | P |
| N | R | E | W | E | I | Q | Z | E | T | G | R | V | A | M |
| O | I | N | Q | N | M | S | K | M | I | S | I | G | H | A |
| V | N | Y | E | C | E | C | T | S | P | E | I | X | C | P |
| E | T | A | B | W | N | W | T | I | W | U | A | G | L | P |
| R | P | A | I | C | T | R | T | Z | N | W | U | B | E | Z |
| N | Y | T | I | L | A | N | O | I | T | A | N | B | T | R |
| I | V | F | D | T | R | I | N | N | K | P | T | D | O | D |
| G | I | M | I | N | Y | V | U | W | P | J | N | I | H | C |
| H | S | O | F | A | C | I | L | I | T | I | E | S | O | T |
| T | N | K | S | E | D | T | N | O | R | F | J | P | H | N |

## 6-1 PAIR WORK

O STUDENT A

| RESERVATION CLERK | GUEST |
|---|---|
| Welcome to **Four Seasons**. May I help you? | Yes. I'd like a room, please. |
| What kind of room would you like? | I'd like a **twin** room. How much is it? |
| It's $**285** net. May I have your name, please? | Okay. My name is **Tom Jones**. |
| How do you spell your family name? | **J-O-N-E-S**. |
| How many are in your party? | There are **2**. |
| How many nights would you like to stay? | Just **1** night. |
| How will you be paying, **Mr. Jones**? | I'll pay by **Visa**. |
| Would you like a wake-up call? | Yes. At **7:15**, please. |
| Your room number is **818**. It is on the **8th** floor. Here's your key card. | Thanks a lot. |

**Part One:** You are a RESERVATION CLERK.
Take a reservation of a Walk-in Guest and fill in the chart below.

**Marriott Hotel**

| TYPE | PRICE | ROOMS AVAILABILITY |
|---|---|---|
| Single | $135 | #204/607/1330/1770 |
| Double | $165 | #101/930/913/1220 |
| Suite | $330 | #1120/1550/2112 |

Note: Check-out time: 11:00 A.M.

| Guest Name | Room Type | No. of Guest(s) | No. of Night(s) | Wake-up Call (time) | Payment |
|---|---|---|---|---|---|
| | | | | | |

**Part Two:** You are a WALK-IN GUEST. Make a reservation.
Fill out the price and check-out time below.

| Guest Name | Room Type | No. of Guest(s) | No. of Night(s) | Wake-up Call (time) | Payment |
|---|---|---|---|---|---|
| Peter Smith | Double | 2 | Overnight | Yes. At 6:15 | Diners' Club |

Price: ___________
Check-out Time: ___________

## ⑥-2 PAIR WORK

**○ STUDENT B**

| RESEVATION CLERK | GUEST |
|---|---|
| Welcome to **Four Seasons**. May I help you? | Yes. I'd like a room, please. |
| What kind of room would you like? | I'd like a **twin** room. How much is it? |
| It's $**285** net. May I have your name, please? | Okay. My name is **Tom Jones**. |
| How do you spell your family name? | **J-O-N-E-S**. |
| How many are in your party? | There are **2**. |
| How many nights would you like to stay? | Just **1** night. |
| How will you be paying, **Mr. Jones**? | I'll pay by **Visa**. |
| Would you like a wake-up call? | Yes. At **7:15**, please. |
| Your room number is **818**. It is on the **8th** floor. Here's your key card. | Thanks a lot. |

**Part One:** You are a WALK-IN GUEST. Make a reservation.
Fill out the price and check-out time below.

| Guest Name | Room Type | No. of Guest(s) | No. of Night(s) | Wake-up Call (time) | Payment |
|---|---|---|---|---|---|
| Amanda York | Suite | 1 | A week | Yes. At 7:30 | Amex |

Price: ___________
Check-out Time: ___________

**Part Two:** You are a RESERVATION CLERK.
Take a reservation of a Walk-in Guest and fill in the chart below.

swissôtel
Hotels & Resorts

| TYPE | PRICE | ROOMS AVAILABILITY |
|---|---|---|
| Single | $170 | #310/717/808/1005 |
| Double | $190 | #212/616/911/1330 |
| Suite | $415 | #1414/1880/2012 |

Note: Check-out time: 1:00 P.M.

| Guest Name | Room Type | No. of Guest(s) | No. of Night(s) | Wake-up Call (time) | Payment |
|---|---|---|---|---|---|
| | | | | | |

## 7 READING

# Hotel Room of the Future

1 The Hilton Garden Inn's gadget-crammed Room 267 is not your typical lodging. But stay just one night there, and you'll want it to be. The invitation-only "Room of the Future" is in a special Hilton University wing of the property near Los Angeles International Airport. It comes furnished with a lot of next-generation products to enhance guests' comfort. Among the features of this high-tech hotel room are:

- a 42-inch flat-screen HDTV plasma television with surround sound speakers.
- a biometric room safe that uses a thumbprint as the lock and key;
- free broadband, accessible via laptop or the TV.
- a touch-panel remote control that adjusts lighting levels and room climate; opens and closes the drapes; controls the TV, radio and DVD player.
- a massage chair, a heated toilet seat/bidet, a computerized five-nozzle shower, and a defogging bathroom mirror.

2 The bathroom, which has a glassed-in shower, offers five nozzles and computerized water-temperature control. While it sounds luxurious, it proves more annoying than enjoyable. First, guests need 20/20 vision to deal with the many controls. If they press the wrong button 102-degree water comes blasting out. (Hilton plans to install a voice-activated control) Despite all the high-end design, the shower lacks a soap dish.

3 The Jacuzzi bath has an overhead flat-panel TV. The TV shows only whatever channel is playing on the TV in the bedroom; no switching from the bathroom.

4 The king size bed does not have a mattress, but a system of air pockets instead of springs. The head, foot, and left and right sides of the bed go up and down via remote controls at each side--great for sitting up to read and to watch TV.

5 This is the hotel room of the future. Would you like to check it out?

## COMPREHENSION

◆ **Answer the questions using complete sentences.**

**1.** What do you think the most interesting feature of the hotel room is?

**2.** What hotel chain can you find this "room of the future" in?

**3.** Name 2 features of the bathroom that should be changed.

**4.** What are some high tech features of the bed?

**5.** What state can you find this hotel room in?

## 8 ONE MORE TIME

◆ **Make groups of three. The group leader chooses a category and tells the group whether the category is a Service, a Place, a Person, or a Thing. S/He then reads the clues. The group will try to guess what it is. Whoever guesses it right gets to select a different category.**

### Guess What...?

| (1) A PERSON | (2) A SERVICE |
|---|---|
| Opposite of run out<br>In person check-in<br>Type of hotel guest<br>Depends on availability<br>No advance reservation made | Breakfast<br>Shuttle bus<br>Free service<br>Fruit basket in a room<br>Airport pick-up/drop-off |

| (3) A SERVICE | (4) A PLACE | (5) A THING |
|---|---|---|
| Get up early<br>A phone call<br>A special request<br>Occurs in the morning<br>A request made at the reception | Check-in<br>Check-out<br>Ask for an extra key<br>Make reservations<br>Request information | Big<br>Expensive<br>Luxurious<br>Has a living room<br>A type of hotel room |

| (6) A PLACE | (7) A THING |
|---|---|
| Type of facilities<br>Large space<br>Found in a hotel<br>For business meetings<br>A kind of function room | Fill-in<br>Check-in<br>A form or card<br>Contains your address<br>Requires one's signature |

| (8) A THING | (9) A PERSON | (10) A THING |
|---|---|---|
| A document<br>Has a picture<br>Has personal information<br>Required to travel overseas<br>Issued by your own country | A job<br>Drives<br>Limousine<br>Wears a uniform<br>Opens car doors | A date<br>Month/Year<br>Has a time limit<br>No longer valid<br>Can be found on credit card |

**STRUCTURE:**
**Leader:** The category is "**A PERSON**".
**A:** Tell us the clues.
**Leader:** All right. **S/He works in a hotel. S/He carries bags.**
**B:** Oh, I know. **Is the person a doorman**?
**Leader:** I'm afraid you are wrong. Try again!
**A: Is s/he a(an) bellboy**?
**Leader:** Yes, that's correct.

# Chapter 8

## *Bon Appetite!*

## ❶ KEY VOCABULARY

| | | | |
|---|---|---|---|
| Appetizer | Pitcher | Side Dish | Set Menu |
| Entrée | Refill | Aperitif | Vegetarian |
| Recommend | Seafood | A la carte | Grill |
| Fillet | Brunch | Napkin | Baked |
| American Breakfast | Carafe | Specials | Homemade |
| Continental Breakfast | Keg | Beverage | Well Done |

## ❷ WARM-UP

➢ **Put the items in the correct place on the Menu. Think of an extra item and price.**

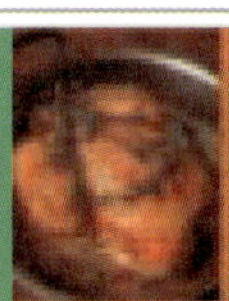

GRAMERCY TAVERN

| | | | |
|---|---|---|---|
| | **Appetizers:** | | |
| ________ | $11.00 | ________ | $14.00 |
| ________ | $____ | ________ | $15.00 |
| | **Entree** | | |
| ________ | $21.00 | ________ | $____ |
| ________ | $23.00 | ________ | $25.00 |
| | **Side Dish** | | |
| ________ | $____ | ________ | $7.25 |
| ________ | $5.85 | ________ | $8.75 |
| | **Drinks** | | |
| ________ | $8.25 | ________ | $5.50 |
| ________ | $____ | ________ | $3.95 |
| | **Desserts** | | |
| ________ | $11.00 | ________ | $5.95 |
| ________ | $7.50 | ________ | $____ |

| | | | | |
|---|---|---|---|---|
| Salmon | Martini | Shrimp Cocktail | Asparagus Soup | Herbal Tea |
| Sorbets | Apple Strudel | Venison | Tiramisu | Rice with Saffron |
| Baked Potato | Sautéed Eggplant | Fresh Fruit Juice | Fillet Mignon | Caesars Salad |

## ❸ LANGUAGE STRUCTURE

| FRONT DESK CLERK | GUEST |
|---|---|
| Would you care for some drinks? | Sure, I'd like a glass of red house wine, please. |
| Are you ready to order? | Yes, I am. / No, I'll be ready in a few minutes. |
| What would you like to start with? | Shrimp cocktail, please. |
| What would you like to order for the main course? | I'd like the Fillet Mignon, please. |
| How would you like it done? | I'd like it medium rare. |
| What would you like with that? | I'll have a baked potato with sour cream. |
| Would you care for dessert? | Yes, I'll have lemon sorbets. / No, thank-you. |

**Part One:** **There are many expressions to take an order. Think of other ways and fill in the blanks. The first one is already done for you.**

**Taking Orders**

⇨Are you ready to order?
⇨May I ________ your order?
⇨What can ____ _____ you?
⇨Would you ______ _____ order now?

**Entrée**

⇨What would you like for your main course?
⇨What ______ _______ entrée?
⇨What do you ______ to _______?
⇨What ____ ___ ____ you for the main course?

**Appetizers**

⇨What would you like to start with?
⇨Would you care ___ ___ appetizer?
⇨What _____ of appetizers would you like to have?
⇨How ______ an appetizer?

**Drinks**

⇨Would you care for some drinks?
⇨What would _____ like to _______?
⇨Can I get you _________from the bar?
⇨____you ______ anything to drink?

**Part Two:** **There many different ways to prepare food. Think of other ways and fill in the blanks.**

**Salad Dressings**

- Thousand Islands
- I _ _ _ _ an
- F _ _ _ _ h
- B _ _ e C _ _ _ se

**Potatoes**

- Baked
- M _ _ _ ed
- R _ _ _ ted
- F _ _ _ _ _ F _ _ _ s

**Cooking Methods**

- Grill
- B _ _ _ _ cued
- D _ _ p F _ _ ed
- P _ _ ch

**Eggs**

- Fried
- S _ _ _ _ S _ _ _ U _
- O _ _ _ _ _ _ _ e
- S _ _ _ _ bled

**Meat**

- Medium
- R _ _ e
- M _ _ _ _ _ R _ _ _
- W _ _ _ D _ _ _

**Vegetables**

- Stir fried
- St _ _ _ ed
- Bo _ _ _ d
- R _ _

## 4 CONVERSATION

➢ **Practice the following dialogue with a partner.**

**Mario:** **Are you ready to** order? ①
**Hilary:** Certainly. I'll have the **Fillet Mignon**, please? ❶
**Mario:** How would you like it **cooked**? ②
**Hilary:** I'd like it **medium rare**. ❷
**Mario:** And **what would you like** with that? ③
**Hilary:** I'll have **a baked potato** and mixed vegetables. ❸
**Mario:** Sure. How about an appetizer.
**Hilary:** What do you recommend?
**Mario:** The **onion** soup is today's special. ④
**Hilary:** That sounds perfect. And I'll have a **glass of Fetzer**. ❹
**Mario:** Here's your order, madam. Bon Appetite!
**Hilary:** Waiter…this soup tastes strange. Oh, my goodness! There's something crawling in it.
**Mario:** You're right. There's a cockroach in your soup. I'm very sorry, madam. Let me replace it for you.
**Hilary:** I don't think so. Bring the manger over right away!

## SUBSTITUTION DRILL

➢ **Substitute with the words or phrases below:**

| Mario | Hilary |
|---|---|
| ① May I take your<br>What would you like to<br>What do you want to | ❶ roast beef<br>lamp chops<br>T-Bone steak |
| ② done<br>prepared<br>served | ❷ medium<br>rare<br>well done |
| ③ do you want anything<br>would you like a side order<br>how about something to go | ❸ mashed potatoes<br>some French fries<br>roasted potatoes |
| ④ mushroom<br>tomato<br>chicken noodle | ❹ bottle of beer<br>carafe of red wine<br>Scotch on the rocks |

## 5 CHALLENGE YOURSELF

➢ **Ask and answer the questions below. Then transfer your answers to the appropriate numbered line. After you've finished, Student A reads #1, Student B reads #2, and so forth.**

**Q: Tell me ………… (Read the words in the parenthesis).**

| STUDENTA (SERVER) | STUDENT B (CUSTOMER) |
|---|---|
| **1(a classmate's name) ______** | **2(an insect) ______** |
| **3(a kind of food) ______** | **6(an animal) ______ and (a body part) ______** |
| **5(a vegetable) ______ and (an animal) ______** | **8(an adjective) ______ and (an animal) ______** |
| **9(a snack food) ______** | **10(a color) ______ and (a vegetable) ______** |
| **11(a flower) ______** | **12(a language) ______** |
| **15(a condiment) ______** | **14(an adjective) ______ (a liquid) ______** |
| **17(an insect) ______, (a fruit) ______ (a seafood) ______** | **18(an insect) ______** |
| **21(an expression of surprise) ______ and (an adjective) ______** | **20(a number) ______** |

**STUDENT A (SERVER)**

1Welcome to ______'s Restaurant. Are you ready to order now?
3Okay. Would you like some ______ to go with that?
5I recommend ______ and ______ soup.
7We sure do. What would you like for an entrée?
9Ok. And would you like ______ to go with that?
11Yes, that's our specialty. How about a ______ salad?
13No problem. What would you like to drink?
15Should I put some ______ in it?
17We have ______ pie, ______ cookies and ______ ice-cream.
19Of course. How many pieces would you like?
21______! Well, please have a/an ______ dinner.

**STUDENT B (CUSTOMER)**

2Yes, thanks. I'd like to start with a basket of fried ______.
4Sure. Also, what kind of soup do you recommend?
6Do you have any ______ ______ soup?
8I would like to have a/an ______ ______ steak.
10No, thanks. Do you have any ______ ______ bread?
12Great! May I have some ______ dressing on it?
14I'd like a/an ______ glass of ______.
16Yes, please. Also I like some dessert.
18Do you have any ______ cake?
20Oh, I'll have ______ pieces, please.
22I sure will. Everything sounds so delicious!

## 6-1 PAIR WORK

**STUDENT A**

| SERVER | CUSTOMER |
|---|---|
| Here's your menu. I'll be back to take your order. | Thank-you. |
| May I take your order now, sir/madam? | Yes. I'd like to start with **Calamari**. |
| What would you like as an entrée? | I'll have the **Grilled Fillet Steak medium rare**. |
| Do you want anything with your entrée? | I'd like the **Potato Croquettes** with my meal. |
| How about a dessert? | The **Soufflé** sounds good. |
| Would you care for something to drink? | Please bring me a/an **Ice Tea**. |
| Here's your order. Enjoy your meal! | Thank-you. I'm sure I will. |
| The total of your bill is $**57.20**. | Here's my credit card. |

**Part One:** You are a GUEST. Look at the menu and check (✓) what you want to order. Now order the food from the server.

### APPETIZERS & SOUPS

❐ Soup of the Day $5.00 ❐ Chef's Pate $13.00 ❐ Asparagus Cream Soup $4.00 ❐ Calamari $8.00

### ENTREES

❐ Braised Leg of Lamb $24.00 ❐ Bouillabaisse $19.00 ❐ Grilled Fillet Steak $27.00
❐ Trout with Almonds $23.00 ❐ King Prawns with Garlic $25.00 ❐ Pork Chops with Plum Sauce $22.00

### SIDE ORDERS

❐ Potato Croquettes $3.00 ❐ Broccoli with Hollandaise Sauce $5.00 ❐ String Beans with Butter $4.00

### DESSERTS

❐ Soufflé $10.00 ❐ Banana Split $6.00 ❐ Chocolate Mousse $8.00 ❐ Pecan Pie $7.00

### BEVERAGES

❐ Ice Tea $4.00 ❐ Soft Drinks $3.00 ❐ Shirley Temple $5.00 ❐ Irish Coffee $7.00
❐ Imported Beer $7.00 ❐ Domestic Beer $5.00 ❐ Cocktail $8.00 ❐ Glass of Bordeaux $9.00

**Part Two:** You are a SERVER. Turn to the next page.

## ⑥-2 PAIR WORK

**○ STUDENT B**

| SERVER | CUSTOMER |
|---|---|
| Here's your menu. I'll be back to take your order. | Thank-you. |
| May I take your order now, sir/madam? | Yes. I'd like to start with **Calamari**. |
| What would you like as an entrée? | I'll have the **Grilled Fillet Steak medium rare**. |
| Do you want anything with your entrée? | I'd like the **Potato Croquettes** with my meal. |
| How about a dessert? | The **Soufflé** sounds good. |
| Would you care for something to drink? | Please bring me a/an **Ice Tea**. |
| Here's your order. Enjoy your meal! | Thank-you. I'm sure I will. |
| The total of your bill is $**57.20**. | Here's my credit card. |

**Part One:** You are a SERVER. Take the Guest's order.
To calculate the bill, look at the previous page for pricing.

*Guest Check*

| Quantity | Items Ordered | Price |
|---|---|---|
| ______ | ______________________________ | __________ |
| ______ | ______________________________ | __________ |
| ______ | ______________________________ | __________ |
| ______ | ______________________________ | __________ |
| ______ | ______________________________ | __________ |
| | Sub-Total: | __________ |
| | Tax (10%): | __________ |
| | Total: | __________ |

Note: Tip not included.

*Thank-You!*
*Please Visit Us Again.*

**Part Two:** You are a GUEST. Turn to the previous page.

## 7 READING

### The Ultimate Dining Experience Under the Sea

1 Mr. Ahmed Saleem, one of the Hilton Maldives Resort and Spa's owners, came up with the idea of building an undersea restaurant in 2001 when he was in Bali, having seen a room built into the side of a hill facing a river. Four years later, his dream became reality, when on April 15th; Ithaa Undersea restaurant opened its doors to the first diners.

2 In the Maldivian language of Divehi, "ithaa" means "pearl". The restaurant Ithaa sits like a pearl beneath the waves, between the lagoon and a coral reef. All the walls of the restaurant are transparent, offering 180 degree views of the surrounding marine life and coral reef. The inside of the restaurant is 9 meters long and 5 meters wide.

3 The restaurant's total weight, when it was lowered into the sea was 175 tons with 85 more tons of sand having to be placed inside the structure to sink it into the sea. The total cost of building this restaurant was about US $5 million.

4 Ithaa can seat 14 diners at a time and is reached by a wooden walkway from the nearby Sunset Grill Restaurant. Guests begin their meal with drinks on a specially constructed deck on the surface before descending to the restaurant via a special staircase.

5 Such a unique restaurant deserves a distinctive cuisine, which is why the theme is 'contemporary Maldivian cuisine'. This innovative style takes local spices, seasonings and traditional cooking methods but adds a western twist. Ithaa is the first and only restaurant in the world to offer fusion Madivian cuisine. The menu offers diners the opportunity to discover and experience a combination of flavors and textures.

6 There is one other underwater restaurant, in Eilat, Israel. Several other restaurants claim to be underwater (Dubai, Caribbean) but in fact they are surrounded by an aquarium and are not in open water. Ithaa is the world's first aquarium-style restaurant-truly affording diners stunning views of the surrounding reefs and fish life.

## COMPREHENSION

◆ **One word in each sentence is incorrect. Cross it out and write the correct answer.**

**1.** Ithaa Undersea Restaurant is located in Bali.

**2.** Ithaa comes from French, meaning pearl.

**3.** The seating capacity of Ithaa is twenty.

**4.** Ithaa Restaurant serves Western food.

**5.** Ithaa opened in 2000.

**6.** Guests take an elevator to the restaurant.

## 8 ONE MORE TIME

### *Word Battleship*

**Part One:** Make 2 teams of four people. Each team writes down the following in GRID 1.

GRID 1

| | A | B | C | D | E | F | G | H | I | J | K | L |
|---|---|---|---|---|---|---|---|---|---|---|---|---|
| 1 | | | | | | | | | | | | |
| 2 | | | | | | | | | | | | |
| 3 | | | | | | | | | | | | |
| 4 | | | | | | | | | | | | |
| 5 | | | | | | | | | | | | |
| 6 | | | | | | | | | | | | |
| 7 | | | | | | | | | | | | |
| 8 | | | | | | | | | | | | |
| 9 | | | | | | | | | | | | |
| 10 | | | | | | | | | | | | |
| 11 | | | | | | | | | | | | |
| 12 | | | | | | | | | | | | |

**Use the information below to fill in GRID 1**

- 2 vegetables - horizontally
- 2 types of desserts - vertically
- 2 types of appetizers - vertically
- 2 main courses - horizontally

When you are finished filling in GRID 1

GO TO PART TWO

GRID 2

| | A | B | C | D | E | F | G | H | I | J | K | L |
|---|---|---|---|---|---|---|---|---|---|---|---|---|
| 1 | | | | | | | | | | | | |
| 2 | | | | | | | | | | | | |
| 3 | | | | | | | | | | | | |
| 4 | | | | | | | | | | | | |
| 5 | | | | | | | | | | | | |
| 6 | | | | | | | | | | | | |
| 7 | | | | | | | | | | | | |
| 8 | | | | | | | | | | | | |
| 9 | | | | | | | | | | | | |
| 10 | | | | | | | | | | | | |
| 11 | | | | | | | | | | | | |
| 12 | | | | | | | | | | | | |

**Part Two:** Take turns finding the 8 hidden words that the other group filled in GRID 1. Use the example below to ask and answer each other's questions.

**STRUCTURE:**

Q: Is there a letter in "H9"?
A: No, there isn't.

Q: Is there a letter in "D7"?
A: Yes, there is an "O".

Q: Is there a letter in "C7"?
A: Yes, there is a "P".

Q: Is your hidden word "POTATO"?
A: Yes, it is.

➢ Fill in the GRID with all the words you have guessed correctly.

**NOTE:** The first group to find all the hidden words is the WINNER.

**REMEMBER:** You must find all of the following words in order to win this Word Battleship Game.

⇨ 2 Vegetables ⇨ 2 Desserts
⇨ 2 Appetizers ⇨ 2 Main Courses

# Chapter 9

## *I'm Ready To Check-Out.*

## ❶ KEY VOCABULARY

| | | | |
|---|---|---|---|
| Portfolio | Settle the Bill | International Call | Room Service |
| Overcharged | Amount | Balance | Fax |
| Receipt | Dispute | Miscellaneous | Dry Cleaning |
| Itemized | Feedback | Rented | Mistake |
| Description | Debit | VAT | Transportation |
| Reference Number | Calculate | Rejected | Total Due |

## ❷ WARM-UP

➤ **Work with a partner. Fill in the colored boxes. The first one is already done for you.**

Le ROYAL MERIDIEN BRISTOL

Krakowskie Przedmiescie 42/44, Warsaw, 00-325, Poland

**Mr. Aaron Blake**
**265 Essex Street**
**London, England WC2R 3AA**

① Room Number: 1417
**Arrival:** 08/26/04
**Departure:** 08/27/04
**No. of Guest(s):** 1
**Rate:** 90 Euros ++
② [ ]: 125602

| ③ | ④ | ⑤ | ⑥ | ⑦ |
|---|---|---|---|---|
| 08/26 | IDD – London 18:32 | 7096338004 | 15.80 | 15.80 |
| 08/26 | Business Center – Fax 18:22 | 6052786981 | 4.10 | 19.90 |
| 08/26 | Malinowa Restaurant | 5085496302 | 38.25 | 58.15 |
| 08/26 | Column Bar | 8186855234 | 9.75 | 67.90 |
| 08/26 | Dry Cleaning | 4986536823 | 6.35 | 74.25 |
| 08/26 | Miscellaneous | 9985686540 | 5.65 | 79.90 |
| 08/26 | Transportation | 3198062987 | 20.00 | 99.90 |
| 08/26 | Room Service | 5673489452 | 22.95 | 122.85 |
| 08/26 | Room Charge | 0086954823 | 90.00 | 212.85 |
| 08/26 | Service Charge | 0086695685 | 9.00 | 221.85 |
| 08/26 | VAT | 0086895641 | 14.85 | 236.70 |

⑧ [ ] ➲ **236.70 Euros**

**Thank-you. We look forward to serving you again.**

Signature: *Aaron Blake*

## ❸ LANGUAGE STRUCTURE

| FRONT DESK CLERK | GUEST |
|---|---|
| Are you ready to check-out now? | Yes, I am. My room number is 1417. |
| Okay. Here's your bill. | Thank-you. Can you explain what this item is for? |
| Do you still want to pay by Visa? | Yes, I do. |
| Is your bill correct? | Yes, it is. / No, it isn't. |
| Can you sign here, please? | Of course. |
| I hope you enjoyed your stay with us. | Yes, it was very enjoyable. |

**Part One:** **Fill in the green areas with the correct tense.**

| Present Tense | Past Tense | Present Tense | Past Tense |
|---|---|---|---|
| is ➔ | | say ➔ | |
| | ⇦ arrived | | ⇦ departed |
| do ➔ | | cost ➔ | |
| | ⇦ enjoyed | | ⇦ charged |
| eat ➔ | | see ➔ | |
| have ➔ | | buy ➔ | |
| | ⇦ dry cleaned | | ⇦ rejected |
| make ➔ | | take ➔ | |
| | ⇦ ordered | pay ➔ | |
| send ➔ | | | ⇦ explained |
| | ⇦ rented | come ➔ | |

**Part Two:** **Refer to the bill on the previous page. You are A HOTEL CLERK. Explain the bill to Mr. Blake in the order of the items posted. Fill in the blanks with the correct information.**

**FOR EXAMPLE: You __________ in room ________.**
**(stayed) (1417)**

1. On August 26th you _______________.
2. You _______________ on August 27th.
3. An international call was ________________. The charge _________ 15.80 Euros.
4. A fax was ____________. It ____________ 4.10 Euros.
5. You ________ a meal at the ___________ ___________ and the ________was _____ Euros.
6. On ____________ you __________ a drink at the ____________ __________.
7. Your suit was ______ ________ ______ August 26th.
8. Miscellaneous ___________ ___________ 6.35 Euros.
9. A car ___________ ___________ on August 26th. And it _________ 20 Euros.
10. You ____________ ___________ ___________. And the price was 22.95 Euros.
11. The ___________ ___________ for one night was ________ Euros.
12. 9 Euros was for the _______________ ________________.
13. The _______________ was 14.85 Euros.
14. The ____________ comes out to 236.70 Euros.

## ④ CONVERSATION

➤ **Practice the following dialogue with a partner.**

**Bernard:** I'm ready to **check-out** now. My room number is 1,250. ①
**Murrain:** Okay. Here's your bill, sir. The **balance is** $632.50. Is this correct? ❶
**Bernard:** What?? May I see the bill, please?
**Murrain:** Sure. Here it is.
**Bernard:** Excuse me. Can you explain what **IDD** is for? ②
**Murrain:** You **made an international call to Australia**. ❷
**Bernard:** There seems to be a mistake here. I never **made an international call**. ③
**Murrain:** Well, let me take a look at your bill. Oh, I'm sorry, sir. This bill is for room 1215. Here's your bill.
**Bernard:** Are you sure **this is correct**? I never used the mini-bar. I don't drink. ④
**Murrain:** But **our record** shows that a bottle of champagne is missing. ❸
**Bernard:** Are you joking? I just told you that I don't drink. Oh, no! There's another mistake here. Also, you overcharged me for the room. I was quoted $150 for a single room.
**Murrain:** Our computer shows that the room rate is right.
**Bernard:** I CAN'T BELIEVE THIS?! You call this a 5 star hotel?!
**Murrain:** Let me **get** the manager. ❹

## SUBSTITUTION DRILL

➤ **Substitute with the words or phrases below:**

| Bernard | Murrain |
|---|---|
| ① leave<br>depart<br>go | ❶ total charge is<br>bill comes out to be<br>balance due is |
| ② dry cleaning<br>transportation<br>room service | ❷ had your suit dry cleaned<br>rented a car<br>ordered room service |
| ③ had my suit dry cleaned<br>rented a car<br>ordered room service | ❸ our computer<br>your portfolio<br>our file |
| ④ there isn't a mistake here<br>this bill is right<br>this is my bill | ❹ talk to<br>check with<br>verify it with |

## 5 CHALLENGE YOURSELF

**Part One:** Make a sentence for each word below. The first one is done for you.

| | | | | |
|---|---|---|---|---|
| Overcharged | Rejected | Balance due | Explain | Rented |
| Receipt | VAT | Describe | Dispute | Pay |
| Mistake | Miscellaneous | Ordered | Calculate | Verify |

1. Please wait one moment, sir. I'll **verify** your bill with the manager________________.
2. ________________________________________________.
3. ________________________________________________.
4. ________________________________________________.
5. ________________________________________________.
6. ________________________________________________.
7. ________________________________________________.
8. ________________________________________________.
9. ________________________________________________.
10. ________________________________________________.
11. ________________________________________________.
12. ________________________________________________.
13. ________________________________________________.
14. ________________________________________________.
15. ________________________________________________.

**Part Two:** Read each sentence you wrote in Part One. DO NOT say the word, instead say "blank". Your partner will try to guess the word.

**FOR EXAMPLE:**

A: Please wait one moment, sir. I'll **(blank)** your bill with the manager.
B: Is the word in the blank **verify**?
A: Yes, it is. / No, it isn't. Try again!

## 6-1 PAIR WORK

**STUDENT A**

| CASHIER | GUEST |
|---|---|
| 1. How many nights did you stay?<br>**Your total room charge is $ _____.** | I stayed for ____ night(s). |
| 2. What did you order from room service?<br>**The price of the room service comes to $_____.** | I ordered a ___________. |
| 3. What did you have dry cleaned?<br>**The cost of the dry cleaning is $_____.** | I had a __________ dry cleaned. |
| 4. What did you have from the mini-bar?<br>**The charge from the mini-bar is $_____.** | I had a ____________. |
| 5. How many international calls did you make?<br>**Your international calls cost $_______.** | I made _____ calls. |
| 6. What did you eat at the restaurant?<br>**Your restaurant bill is $_______.** | I had ____________. |
| 7. What did you use at the business center?<br>**The cost for using the business center is $______.** | I sent ________ faxes to Madrid. |

**Part One:** You are a CASHIER. Ask your Guest the above questions and check (✓) the box. Calculate the total charges. Use the example in red to explain the bill to your Guest.

| | | | | |
|---|---|---|---|---|
| **Nightly Rate** | | | | |
| ☐ $125<br>One | ☐ $250<br>Two | ☐ $375<br>Three | ☐ $500<br>Four | |
| **Room Service** | | | | |
| ☐ $10.75<br>Hamburger | ☐ $12.85<br>Club Sandwich | ☐ $8.99<br>Chef Salad | ☐ $11.35<br>Pizza | |
| **Dry Cleaned** | | | | |
| ☐ $10.40<br>Suit | ☐ $3.55<br>Shirt | ☐ $6.10<br>Skirt | ☐ $7.89<br>Jacket | |
| **Mini-Bar** | | | | |
| ☐ $5.49<br>Beer | ☐ $2.05<br>Soda | ☐ $2.45<br>Juice | ☐ $2.29<br>Bag of Peanuts | |
| **IDD** | | | | |
| ☐ $5.00<br>2 calls | ☐ $10.30<br>3 calls | ☐ $15.69<br>4 calls | ☐ $20.12<br>5 calls | |
| **Restaurant** | | | | |
| ☐ $13.39<br>Breakfast | ☐ $18.25<br>Lunch | ☐ $27.59<br>Dinner | ☐ $3.70<br>Coffee/Tea | |
| **Fax** | | | | |
| ☐ $10.96<br>Two | ☐ $16.44<br>Three | ☐ $21.92<br>Four | ☐ $27.40<br>Five | |
| | | | **Sub-Total:** | ______________ |
| | | | **VAT & Service Charge (20%):** | ______________ |
| | | | **Grand Total:** | ______________ |

**Part Two:** You are a GUEST. Turn to the next page.

## 6-2 PAIR WORK

**STUDENT B**

| CASHIER | GUEST |
|---|---|
| 1. How many nights did you stay? | I stayed for **4** night(s). |
| 2. What did you order from room service? | I ordered a **hamburger**. |
| 3. What did you have dry cleaned? | I had a **jacket** dry cleaned. |
| 4. What did you have from the mini-bar? | I had a **beer**. |
| 5. How many international calls did you make? | I made **4** calls. |
| 6. What did you eat at the restaurant? | I had **dinner**. |
| 7. What did you use at the business center? | I sent **3** faxes to Madrid. |

**Part One:** You are a GUEST. Check (✓) 1 box in each of the category. Answer the Cashier's questions. When the Cashier explains the bill to you, write down the charges.

| | | | | | |
|---|---|---|---|---|---|
| **Nightly Rate** | ☐ One | ☐ Two | ☐ Three | ☐ Four | |
| **Room Service** | ☐ Hamburger | ☐ Club Sandwich | ☐ Chef Salad | ☐ Pizza | |
| **Dry Cleaned** | ☐ Suit | ☐ Shirt | ☐ Skirt | ☐ Jacket | |
| **Mini-Bar** | ☐ Beer | ☐ Soda | ☐ Juice | ☐ Bag of Peanuts | |
| **IDD** | ☐ 2 calls | ☐ 3 calls | ☐ 4 calls | ☐ 5 calls | |
| **Restaurant** | ☐ Breakfast | ☐ Lunch | ☐ Dinner | ☐ Coffee/Tea | |
| **Fax** | ☐ Two | ☐ Three | ☐ Four | ☐ Five | |
| | | | | **Sub-Total:** | ________ |
| | | | | **VAT & Service Charge (20%):** | ________ |
| | | | | **Grand Total:** | ________ |

**Part Two:** You are a CASHIER. Turn to the previous page.

## 7 READING

### Sleeping With the Fishes

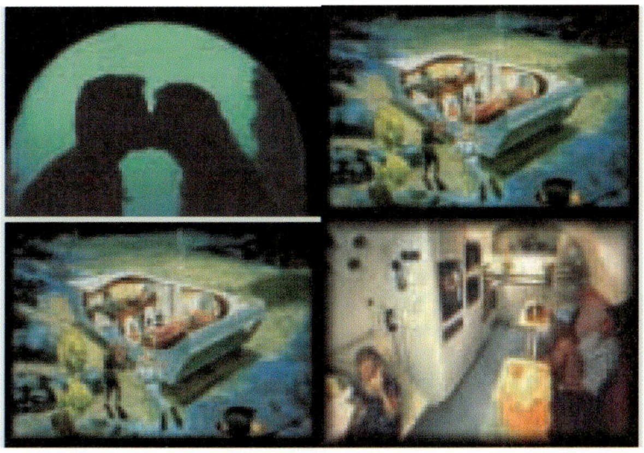

**1** Sleeping underwater sounds like a dream. But modern architects in Key Largo, Florida have made this dream a reality Jules' Undersea Lodge was originally built as a scientific laboratory for ocean research. In 1986 the lodge was redesigned as the world's only underwater hotel.

**2** Guests, who pay $325 a night, arrive in diving suits and enter through a small pool and air lock. Once inside, they breathe normally. Entering through an opening in the bottom of the habitat, the feeling is much like discovering a secret underwater clubhouse," according to the lodge's Web site.

**3** The 600-square-foot building includes air conditioning, hot showers, a well-stocked kitchen, books, music and videos. The 42-inch round windows in the bedrooms and the common room provide a good view of the surrounding sea life. Each of the two 8-by-10 bedrooms is equipped with a telephone, intercom, television, VCR, stereo sound system, small refrigerator and sink, as well as a double bed.

**4** Because of its small size, Jules' Undersea Lodge resembles a bed and breakfast inn. Although breakfast is not served by an innkeeper, the common room includes a stocked refrigerator and a microwave oven. The staff is on duty 24 hours a day to provide any necessary services. A local shop provides underwater pizza delivery

## COMPREHENSION

◆ **Write T if the sentence is true and F if the sentence is false. If it is false, make it true.**

**1.** Jules' Undersea Lodge is located in Canada. _____

**2.** The Lodge opened its door in 1996. _____

**3.** The room rate is $325 per night. _____

**4.** Guests go diving to reach the hotel. _____

**5.** There are four guest rooms. _____

**6.** Jules' Undersea Lodge was originally an aquarium. _____

**7.** You can order pizza delivery. _____

## 8 ONE MORE TIME

◆ **Divide the class into 2 teams. Decide which team goes first. The first team rolls a die and moves the counter according to the number rolled. The teacher reads out the sentence in that box. If the team can answer the question correctly they get to stay in that box. If their answer is incorrect, they must go back to the previous box. The team that checks-out first is the winner.**

**RECEPTION**

**Greet your guests.**

What does a guest fill out when he arrives?

Another word for one night is this.

Where do you check-in?

What does ++ mean?

What type of room is this?

A business meeting is usually held in this place.

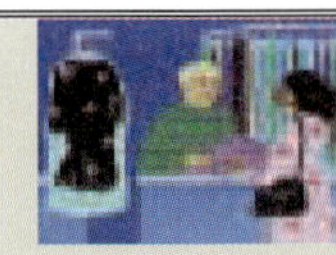

You had your dress __________.

What kind of room would you like?

The amount of the room is this.

Explain this item on the bill.

Please _____ the bill to me.

Name 4 ways to pay your hotel bill.

A person who provides special services to guests.

Who do you call when you want extra towels?

Name 5 hotel facilities.

You were Overcharged.

GO AHEAD 2 SPACES

When you are ready to leave you must do this.

Your shirt is dirty.

GO BACK 3 SPACES.

Who is this person?

Another word for a free hotel service is this.

You lost your key card.

GO BACK TO RECEPTION.

This person drives a limousine.

The total amount before tax is called this.

GO TO CHECK-OUT

Another word for availability is this.

GO AHEAD 2 SPACES

You call this person when you are hungry.

You want to get opera tickets.

GO BACK 10 SPACES

Explain this item on the bill

When your credit card is denied it is this.

**CHECK-OUT**

**Say good-bye to your guests.**

# Chapter 10

## *Place Your Bet!*

## ❶ KEY VOCABULARY

| | | | |
|---|---|---|---|
| Blackjack | Pay-off | Bet | Dealer |
| Roll | VIP | Chips | Even Money |
| Dice | Cash-out | Stand | Odds |
| Roulette | Spin | Hit | Poker |
| Progressive Jackpot | Craps | Slot Machine | Wage |
| Let it Ride | Player | Baccarat | Deck of Cards |

## ❷ WARM-UP

**Part One:** **Can you guess what game each picture represents? Write the name of the game under the appropriate picture. Each game might have 2 pictures.**

A

B

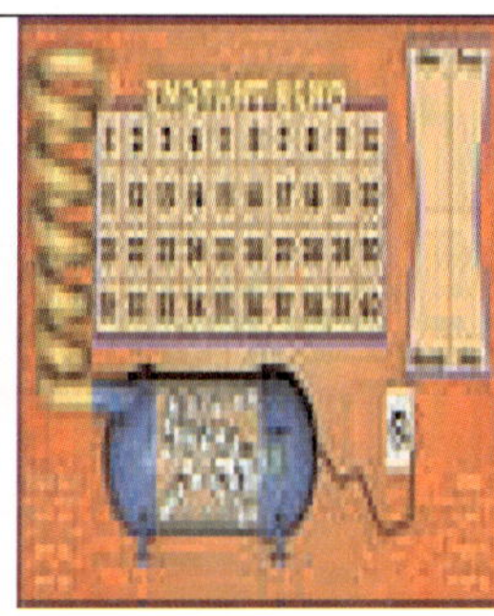

C

D

E

F

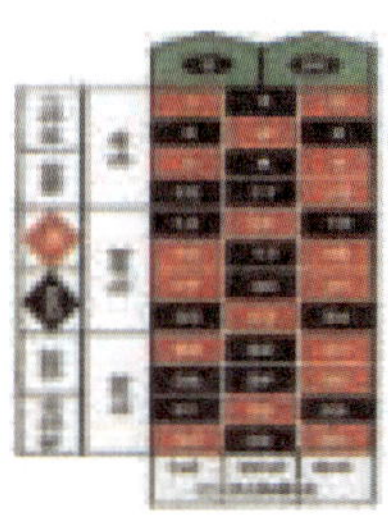

G

H

I

J

**Part Two:** **Compare your answers with a partner. Use the given structure below.**

**FOR EXAMPLE:**

**A: What game do you think Picture A represents?**
**B: I think the game is ____________. And what do you think?**

## ❸ LANGUAGE STRUCTURE

| PLAYER | CASINO DEALER |
|---|---|
| Can I change $20 worth of chips, please? | Certainly. Here are your chips. |
| What is the maximum table bet? | The maximum table bet is a $100. |
| How much did I win on my bet? | You won $250. |
| Could you place $25 on number 24 for me? | Sure. Put your chips on the table first. |
| When can I place my bet? | You can place it now. |
| May I cash-out my chips now? | Yes, you can bring them to the cashier. |
| What is the pay-out for a Flush? | It is 5 to 1. |

➢ **Write down the name of the game in the green areas using the list below.**

| A | B | C | D |
|---|---|---|---|
| ◆ "Shooter" throws the dice.<br>◆You win if the 1st throw is 7 or 11, but lose if it is 2,3 or 12.<br>◆ Types of wages includes: Pass Line, Come Bets, Odds, Place Bets, Field Bets and Hard Ways.<br>◆ Pass Line pays even money.<br>◆ Come Bets makes this game exciting. | ◆ This game is the most popular casino table card game.<br>◆ The object of this game is to have your cards total higher than the dealer's hand, without going over 21.<br>◆ 21 on your first two cards pays 1 ½ times your bet. Here you can not lose, but can tie with the dealer.<br>◆ Hit and Stand are some words used in this game.<br>◆ This game has the following options: Splitting-Pairs, Doubling Down, Insurance and Surrender. | ◆ The wheel has black and red numbers 1-36 and the symbols "0" and "00" which are green.<br>◆ Wages can be placed on individual numbers or groups of numbers.<br>◆ If you place your bet on a single number (straight-up), the pay-out is 35-1. Bets on either black or red, pays even money (1-1). Odd and even bets also pay 1-1. Placing your bet on either 1-18; or 19-36, the pay-out is even.<br>◆ You can place your bet until the dealer announces "No more bets".<br>◆ The chips in this game are different from other casino chips. | ◆ This is a 5-card game which matches your hand with the dealers.<br>◆ In this game the dealer also receives 5 cards and only exposes the first card face up.<br>◆ You have a chance to hit a Progressive Jackpot for an additional $1.<br>◆ Some players hand include Pairs, Two Pairs, Three of a Kind, Straight, Flush, Full House, Four of a Kind, Straight Flush and Royal Flush.<br>◆ A simple game that offers you a chance for a big Pay-Off. |

**Roulette** **Baccarat** **Keno** **Blackjack** **Lucky 7**

**Let It Ride** **Pai Gow Poker** **Slot Machine** **Caribbean Stud Poker**

## ④ CONVERSATION

➤ **Practice the following dialogue with a partner.**

**Player:** Can I **change** $1000 worth of chips, please? ①
**Dealer:** Of course. Here are your chips. Good luck!
**Player:** What is the **minimum** table bet? ②
**Dealer:** The **minimum bet is a $100**. This is a VIP table. ❶
**Player:** Today is my 30th birthday. Could you place $500 on number 30 for me, please?
**Dealer:** Certainly. Put your chips on the table first and I'll place it for you on number 13.
**Player:** Okay. I feel very lucky already!
**Dealer:** Alright. Everyone you may place your bets now. (Dealer spins the ball)
No more bets! … And the winning number is …30 RED.
**Player:** Oh, I WON! I WON! **How much do I get** on a $500 bet? ③
**Dealer:** No, I'm afraid **you get nothing**. ❷
**Player:** What do you mean **I get nothing**? My number just came up. Look at the wheel!
Isn't that number 30? ④
**Dealer:** Yes, **it is**. But your chips were on number 13. ❸
**Player:** No?! What do you mean 13? I asked you to place $500 on number 30.
**Dealer:** Well, then. Let's check **the surveillance camera**. ❹

## SUBSTITUTION DRILL

➤ **Substitute with the words or phrases below:**

| Player | Dealer |
|---|---|
| ① get<br>have<br>buy | ❶ maximum bet is a $1000<br>lowest bet is a $100<br>highest bet is a $1000 |
| ② maximum<br>lowest<br>highest | ❷ you just lost<br>your chips were on the wrong number<br>you placed the wrong bet |
| ③ What is the pay-out<br>How much do I win<br>How much do I make | ❸ I can see that<br>I know<br>you are right |
| ④ I just lost<br>my chips were on the wrong number<br>I placed the wrong bet | ❹ with the security camera upstairs<br>with my pit boss<br>the video tape |

## ❺ CHALLENGE YOURSELF

**Part One:** **Match the letters (A-K) with the Roulette terminology.**

**ODD or EVEN** **All odd or even numbers:**
➢ **The pay out is 1 to 1.** ________

**STREET** **Any of the three numbers in the row:**
➢ **The pay out is 11 to 1.** ________

**FIRST FIVE** **0, 00, 1, 2, and 3:**
➢ **The pay out is 6 to 1.** ________

**STRAIGHT-UP** **All numbers, 0 and 00:**
➢ **The pay out is 35 to 1.** ________

**CORNER** **Any of the four numbers forming the corner:** ➢ **The pay out is 8 to 1.** ________

**RED or BLACK** **The color on the number corresponds to the color bet:**
➢ **The pay out is 1 to 1.** ________

**DOUBLE STREET** **Any of the numbers in the two rows bet:** ➢ **The pay out is 5 to 1.** ________

**COLUMN** **Any of the numbers in the Column:** ➢ **The pay out is 2 to 1.** _______

**SPLIT** **Either of the two numbers split:**
➢ **The pay out is 17 to 1.** ________

**DOZEN** **1 through 12 or 13 through 24, or 25 through 36:** ➢ **The pay out is 2 to 1.** ________

**ALL NUMBERS** **1 through 18 or 19 through 36:**
➢ **The pay out is 1 to 1.** ________

ROULETTE TABLE

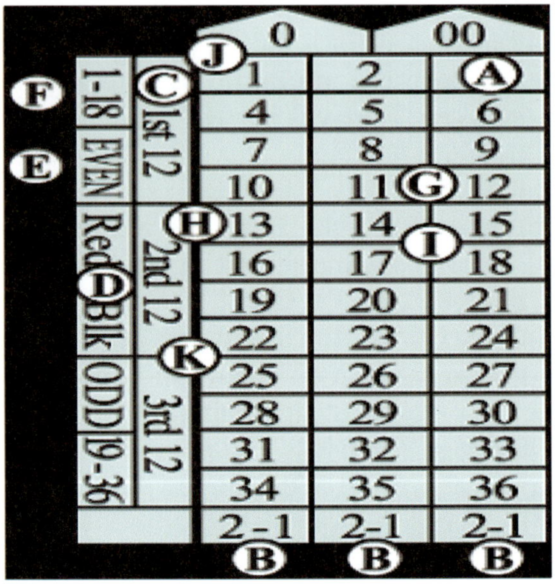


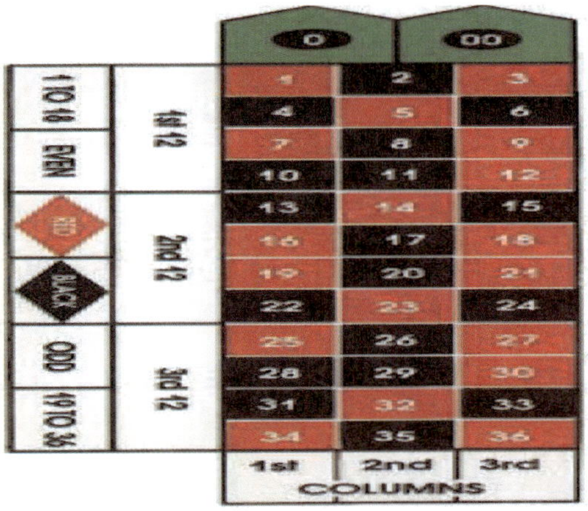


**Part Two:** **Use the above terminology to fill in the green areas. Then calculate the pay-out.**

**Now make groups of four. Take turns asking and answering the questions. The first person to answer the questions correctly gets a point.**

**A: I put a $100 chip on a <u>Column bet</u>. How much was my pay out?**
**B: I think you won <u>$200</u>.**

1) A player made a $10 on a/an ____________ bet. His pay out was $_____________.
2) A $20 bet was placed on a/an _______________ bet. The winnings were $______________.
3) You put $50 on a/n _______________ bet. How much did you win? I won $_____________.
4) Your girlfriend asked you to bet $15. You put it on a/an ________bet. You received $________.
5) It was your lucky day. You placed $30 on a/an _________bet. The dealer gave you $_________.
6) You handed a $1chip to the dealer to put on a/an _____________. The pay was $____________.

## 6-1 PAIR WORK

**O STUDENT A**

| PLAYER | DEALER |
|---|---|
| What's the name of the game? | It's **Blackjack**. |
| Picture 5, what's the name of the player's hand? | It's Double Down. |
| How much is the bet? | The bet is $**25**. |
| What's the pay-off? | The pay-off is **1 to 1**. |
| Is the total winning … $**75**? | No, it isn't. Please re-calculate. |
| Oh, okay. I think the total winning is $**50**, right? | Yes, you're correct. |

**Part One:** You are a DEALER. Use the information below to answer the questions.

**BLACKJACK**

| Picture No. | Player's Hand | Bet | Pay-Off | Total Winning |
|---|---|---|---|---|
| 1 | Split | $25 | 1 to 1 (on each hand) | $50 |
| 2 | Blackjack | $50 | 1 ½ to 1 | $75 |
| 3 | Double Down | $20 plus $20 | 1 to 1 (of total bet) | $40 |
| 4 | 17-Player;22-Dealer (Dealer Busts) | $30 | 1 to 1 | $30 |

**Part Two:** You are a PLAYER. Ask the Dealer for information to complete the chart.

________________ (Name of the Game)

| | 1 | 2 | 3 | 4 |
|---|---|---|---|---|
| | 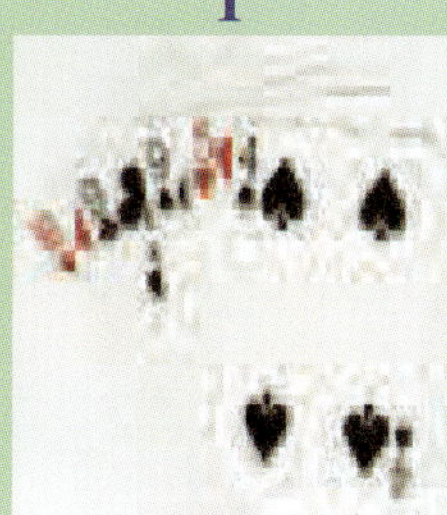 |  |  | 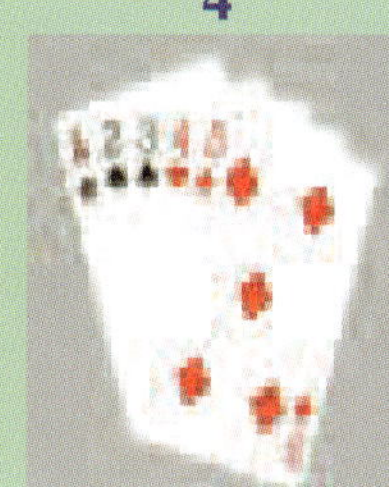 |
| Player's Hand: | | | | |
| Bet (Wage): | | | | |
| Pay-Off: | | | | |
| Total Winning: | | | | |

## 6-2 PAIR WORK

○ STUDENT B

| PLAYER | DEALER |
|---|---|
| What's the name of the game? | It's **Blackjack**. |
| Picture 5, what's the name of the player's hand? | It's a Double Down. |
| How much is the bet? | The bet is $**25**. |
| What's the pay-off? | The pay-off is **1 to 1**. |
| Is the total winning … $**75**? | No, it isn't. Please re-calculate. |
| Oh, okay. I think the total winning is $**50**, right? | Yes, you're correct. |

**Part One:** You are a PLAYER. Ask the Dealer for information to complete the chart.

____________________ (Name of the Game)

| | 1 | 2 | 3 | 4 |
|---|---|---|---|---|
| |  |  | 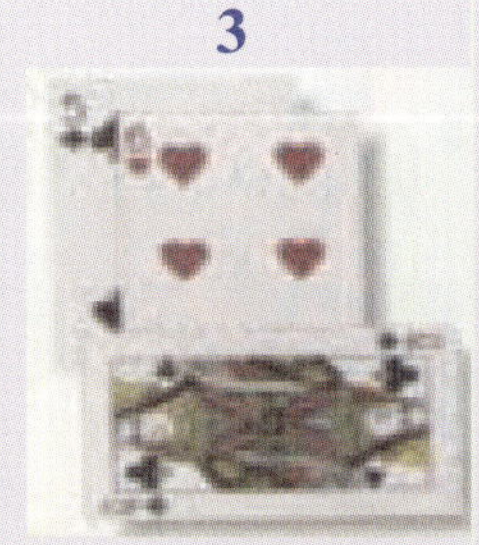 |  |
| Player's Hand: | | | | |
| Bet (Wage): | | | | |
| Pay-Off: | | | | |
| Total Winning: | | | | |

**Part Two:** You are a DEALER. Use the information below to answer the questions.

POKER

| Picture No. | Player's Hand | Bet | Pay-Off | Total Winning |
|---|---|---|---|---|
| 1 | Pair | $15 | 1 to 1 | $15 |
| 2 | Full House | $40 | 7 to 1 | $280 |
| 3 | Flush | $10 | 5 to 1 | $50 |
| 4 | Straight | $50 | 4 to 1 | $200 |

## 7 READING

### "One Armed Bandits"

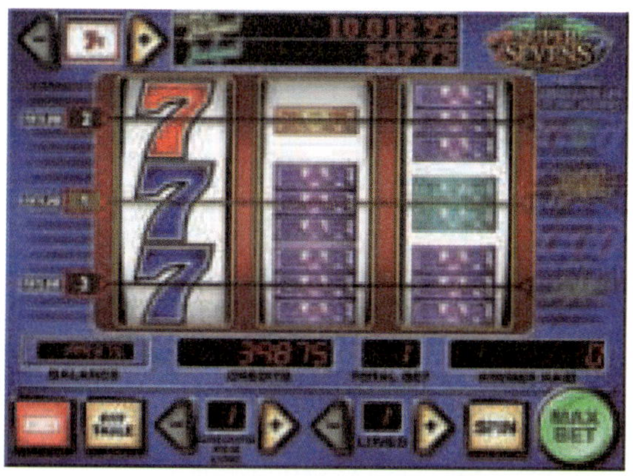


1 Slot machines are a very simple concept. Insert your coin(s), pull the handle and line up matching symbols. You either win or lose! Gamblers are attracted to the slot machines because it is exciting.

2 The first mechanical slot machine was the Liberty Bell, invented in 1895 by Charles Fey, a San Francisco car mechanic. Fey's slot machine had three spinning reels, with diamonds, spades, hearts and one cracked Liberty Bell painted around each reel. Three bells in a row produced the biggest payoff, a grand total of fifty cents or ten nickels. Charles Fey's slot machines were a huge success. He couldn't build them fast enough in his small shop.

3 You might think that casinos make most of their money from the high rollers playing craps, blackjack or baccarat. You would be wrong. More money is bet on slot machines than all the table games combined. One reason for this is because slot machines require no skill and are played at the player's pace. In the early days there were just a few slot machines off in a corner of the casino. Today, most of the casino floor is dedicated to slots.

4 The slot machines today are designed for all budgets from pennies to $500.The choices are almost endless. You can play one line at a time or nine lines at once. Do you like those spinning reels or is a video display more fun? Bells, chimes, and music are among the sounds you can choose from. There are machines that will even talk to you.

## COMPREHENSION

◆ **Match the words in Column A and Column B to make sentences.**

| ANSWERS | A | B |
|---|---|---|
| ______ | **1.** Gamblers like slot machines because | **a.** most of their money on slots. |
| ______ | **2.** The first slot machine | **b.** a car mechanic. |
| ______ | **3.** Casinos make | **c.** is dedicated to slot machines. |
| ______ | **4.** Most of the casino floor | **d.** it is exciting and easy to play. |
| ______ | **5.** Slot machines were invented by | **e.** 9 lines a once. |
| ______ | **6.** You can play one line at a time or | **f.** had 3 spinning wheels. |

## 8 ONE MORE TIME

◆ **Divide the class into 3 teams. 1 student is a Host. The others are Contestants. The Host will draw 4 empty boxes on the blackboard–1 box is for "Used-up Letters" and 3 "Score Boxes" for the Contestants. The Host must keep track of the scores and the used-up letters. The 3 Contestants compete with each other to solve the puzzles. Whoever receives the most cash at the end is the winner.**

◆ **Roll the dice. Choose any letter (other than a vowel). If the letter is in the puzzle, you get the cash and roll again. If the letter isn't in the puzzle, the other player rolls the dice. You can only solve the puzzle on your turn. If you are right, you get the cash. But if your guess is wrong, you loose your turn. Follow the directions in the box below.**

| Directions | Total Roll | Cash ($) |
|---|---|---|
| Double your money | 4 | X2 (of your total cash) |
| Bankrupt | 7 | 0 |
| Loose a turn | 9 | 0 |
| Get one free vowel | 10 | |
| All other numbers | 2, 3, 5, 6, 8, 11, 12 | **Face value** of the dice X $**100** dollars<br>e.g., 5 X $100 = $500 dollars |

**PUZZLE 1**

**PUZZLE 2**

**PUZZLE 3**

**STRUCTURE:**

**H:** It's time to play Wheel of Fortune. **Contestant A**, please roll the dice…each correct letter is worth $**500**.
**C:** Is there a(an) **S** in the puzzle?
**H:** Yes, there are **2 S's**. You have $**1000**. Do you want to solve the puzzle or roll again?
**C:** It's too early to solve it. I'll roll again … Is there a(an) **N** in the puzzle?
**H:** I'm sorry. There aren't any **N's**. **Contestant B**, it's your turn to roll the dice.

---

**H: Host C: Contestant**

# Chapter 11

*We Don't Fly To Chicago.*

## ❶ KEY VOCABULARY

| | | | |
|---|---|---|---|
| Transit | Special Request | Non-Stop/Direct Flight | Booking Class |
| Code-Share | Waitlist | Stopover | Coach |
| Alliance | Open Ticket | Roundtrip | Validity |
| Connecting Flight | High/Low Season | One Way | Outward Flight |
| Return Flight | Reservation number | Fuel Surcharge | Reconfirm |
| Travel Insurance | E-Ticket | Airport Tax | Standby |

## ❷ WARM-UP

Horizon Travel

**AIRLINE RESERVATION FORM**

| Title: Mr./Ms./ Mrs./Dr. | Surname | Given Name | Contact No. | Form of Payment | Travel Insurance | RVSN. No. |
|---|---|---|---|---|---|---|
| **Mr.** | Pearson | Randy | 212-265-7029 | Visa | Yes | CH6LVW |
| **Dr.** | Walker | Jodi | 516-267-6753 | MasterCard | Yes | BF4TZM |
| | | | | | | |
| | **Destination** | **Airline** | **Class** | **Departure** | **Return** | **Status** |
| | **CDG** | **AF** | **C** | **3/15** | **4/12** | **OK** |

➢ **Look at the Reservation Form. Answer the questions.**

1. How many passengers booked the flight? ______________________________
2. How does Dr. Walker pay for her ticket? ______________________________
3. Does Mr. Pearson want travel insurance? ______________________________
4. Where do the passengers want to go? ______________________________
5. What airline do they prefer? ______________________________
6. What do you think "C" class means? ______________________________

➢ **Ask your partner the following questions.**

1. Where do you think "CDG" is located?
2. What airline is "AF"?
3. What does "OK" mean?

## ❸ LANGUAGE STRUCTURE

| TRAVEL AGENT | PASSENGER |
|---|---|
| What is your destination? | I want to go to Cape Town. |
| Would you like a roundtrip ticket? | Yes, I would. |
| When are you leaving? | I'm leaving on the 1st of July. |
| When are you returning? | I'm coming back on the 26th of July. |
| What class do you prefer? | I prefer Coach class. |
| What airline do you prefer? | I'd like South African Airways. |
| Do you need travel insurance? | Yes, I do. |

➢ **Look at the airline timetable. Choose where you want to visit. Use the language structure above and ask four classmates. Record their answers in the chart below. Tell the class which destination is the most popular according to your survey.**

| Destination | Flight # | Departure (ETD) | Arrival (ETA) | Departure |
|---|---|---|---|---|
| **ASIA** | | | | |
| **Hong Kong** | OZ 301 | 09:00 | 11:50 | Daily |
| | CX 411 | 15:35 | 18:10 | Daily |
| **Tokyo** | NW 006 | 09:15 | 11:25 | Friday |
| | JL 958 | 13:40 | 11:40 | M/W/F/S/SU |
| **OCEANIA** | | | | |
| **Sydney** | QF 368 | 20:00 | 07:10 +1 | Daily |
| | KE 811 | 20:40 | 07:40 +1 | Daily |
| **Auckland** | NZ 4207 | 19:30 | 09:40 +1 | M/W/F |
| | KE 823 | 21:15 | 11:30 +1 | Daily |
| **EUROPE** | | | | |
| **Frankfurt** | OZ 541 | 12:40 | 17:00 | M/W/F/SU |
| | LH 713 | 14:35 | 18:30 | Daily |
| **Rome** | KE 8927 | 13:00 | 17:55 | T/TH |
| | AZ 7685 | 13:05 | 18:00 | M/F/SU |
| **NORTH AMERICA** | | | | |
| **Vancouver** | SQ 018 | 18:15 | 12:15 | M/TH/S |
| | AC 064 | 17:10 | 11:20 | Daily |
| **New York** | DL 7855 | 11:00 | 11:40 | Daily |
| | UA 800 | 11:05 | 16:30 | Daily |

**POPULAR DESTINATION SURVEY**

| Student Name | Destination | Leaving (Date) | Returning (Date) | Class | Airline |
|---|---|---|---|---|---|
| 1. | | | | | |
| 2. | | | | | |
| 3. | | | | | |
| 4. | | | | | |

## ❹ CONVERSATION

➢ **Practice the following dialogue with a partner.**

**Airline Agent:** Good afternoon, Air France. How may I help you?
**Mr. Pearson:** Yes, I'd like to **check** my reservation, please. ❶
**Airline Agent:** May I have your **confirmation** number? ①
**Mr. Pearson:** It's CH6LVW.
**Airline Agent:** I'm sorry, Mr. Pearson. But your **reservation** has been cancelled. ②
**Mr. Pearson:** Cancelled? Why? But **I have the ticket right here in my hand**.
I'm supposed to be leaving tomorrow afternoon. ❷
**Airline Agent:** Horizon Travel never **informed** us that they issued your ticket. ③
**Mr. Pearson:** The ticket has already been **paid for**. I have to leave by tomorrow. ❸
**Airline Agent:** Let me check to see if there are any **available** seats on this flight....
Sorry, this flight is full. The next available flight is on March 20th. ④
**Mr. Pearson:** March 20th? **Is there any way you can put me** on the waitlist? ❹
**Airline Agent:** I'm sorry. But the waitlist has been closed. I'd suggest that you contact Horizon Travel.
**Mr. Pearson:** You bet I will!!! They will certainly hear from me.

## SUBSTITUTION DRILL

➢ **Substitute with the words or phrases below:**

| Mr. Pearson | Airline Agent |
|---|---|
| ❶ confirm<br>verify<br>double check | ① reservation<br>record locater<br>reference |
| ❷ I bought the ticket already<br>I picked up the ticket already<br>the ticket has been issued | ② booking<br>seat<br>ticket |
| ❸ charged to my Visa<br>debited from my account<br>paid | ③ told<br>notified<br>mentioned to |
| ❹ Can I be placed<br>Would it be possible to put my name<br>Could you place me | ④ free<br>vacant<br>empty |

## 5 CHALLENGE YOURSELF

➤ **Work with a partner. Look at the airline ticket.**

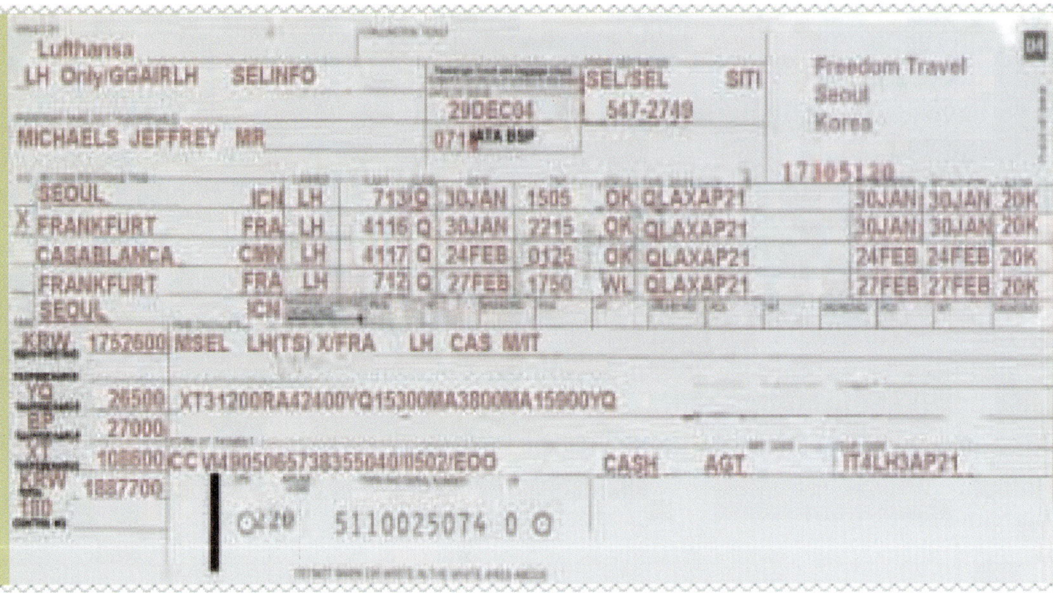

Lufthansa
LH Only/GGAIRLH SELINFO
SEL/SEL SITI
29DEC04 547-2749
MICHAELS JEFFREY MR
071 IATA BSP
Freedom Travel
Seoul
Korea
17305120

| | | | | | | | | | | | |
|---|---|---|---|---|---|---|---|---|---|---|---|
| | SEOUL | ICN | LH | 713 | Q | 30JAN | 1505 | OK | QLAXAP21 | 30JAN | 30JAN | 20K |
| X | FRANKFURT | FRA | LH | 4116 | Q | 30JAN | 2215 | OK | QLAXAP21 | 30JAN | 30JAN | 20K |
| | CASABLANCA | CMN | LH | 4117 | Q | 24FEB | 0125 | OK | QLAXAP21 | 24FEB | 24FEB | 20K |
| | FRANKFURT | FRA | LH | 712 | Q | 27FEB | 1750 | WL | QLAXAP21 | 27FEB | 27FEB | 20K |
| | SEOUL | ICN | | | | | | | | | | |

KRW 1752600 MSEL LH(TS) X/FRA LH CAS MIT
YQ 26500 XT31200RA42400YQ15300MA3800MA15900YQ
BP 27000
XT 108600 CC VI4905065738355040/0502/EOO CASH AGT IT4LH3AP21
KRW 1887700
100
0220 5110025074 0 0

**Lufthansa Airline**

**Class Codes:**

**First Class**
F, A

**Business Class**
C, D, Z

**Economy Class**
Y, B, M, H, Q,
V, W, S, G, K

➤ **Ask your partner the following questions and write down the answers.**

| STUDENT A | STUDENT B |
|---|---|
| **1.** Who issued the ticket? ______ | **11.** When did the passenger depart/return? ______ |
| **2.** To whom was the ticket issued? ______ | **12.** Where was the final destination? ______ |
| **3.** Was this a roundtrip or one-way ticket? ______ | **13.** What was the baggage allowance? ______ |
| **4.** When was the ticket issued? ______ | **14.** What was the status from Frankfurt to Seoul? ______ |
| **5.** Was this a transferable ticket? ______ | **15.** What is the airport code for Casablanca? ______ |
| **6.** Was this a direct flight? ______ | **16.** What does "X" stand for? ______ |
| **7.** What was the ticket number? ______ | **17.** How much was the total airfare? ______ |
| **8.** What class did the passenger fly? ______ | **18.** What was the total tax on this ticket? ______ |
| **9.** What airline did the passenger fly? ______ | **19.** In what currency did the passenger pay for the ticket? ______ |
| **10.** What city did the passenger depart from? ______ | **20.** How did the passenger pay for the ticket? ______ |

## 6-1 PAIR WORK

**STUDENT A**

| AIRLINE AGENT | TRAVEL AGENT |
| --- | --- |
| Good afternoon **Singapore Airlines**. | Good afternoon. This is **Linda Lockhart** from Horizon Travel. |
| How may I help you? | Do you have a flight to **Ottawa** on **April 17**? |
| Yes, we have 2 flights on that date. Do you want the **5:40 a.m.** or the **17:25** flight? | I'd like to reserve a seat on the **17:25** flight. |
| Can I have the passenger's name, please? | The passenger's name is **Frank Johnson**. How much is the airfare? |
| It is **$1,510** plus taxes. | Can I have the reservation number, please? |
| Of course. The reservation number is **CZ 7TLV**. | Thank-you. |
| OR | |
| No, we don't fly to that city. | What airline flies there? |
| **Lufthansa** goes there. | Okay. Thank-you. |

**Part One:** You are a TRAVEL AGENT. Use the chart below to fill in the passenger's destination and departure date. Talk to the Airline Agent to book a seat for the passenger. Then fill in the gray areas with the information you receive from the Airline Agent.

**Horizon Travel**

| Passenger's Name | Destination | Departure Date | Time | Airfare | RVSN. No. |
| --- | --- | --- | --- | --- | --- |
| Mr. Peter Adams | | | | | |
| Ms. Samantha Jones | | | | | |
| Mr. Terry Fox | | | | | |
| Ms. Carrie Bradshaw | | | | | |
| Mrs. Sheri O'Toole | | | | | |

| Destination | Departure Date |
| --- | --- |
| Stockholm | June 18th |
| Johannesburg | November 12th |
| Beijing | April 4th |
| Chicago | February 27th |
| Fiji | July 1st |
| Ottawa | September 2nd |
| Prague | December 3rd |

**Part Two:** You are an AIRLINE AGENT. Turn to the next page.

## ❻-2 PAIR WORK

**○ STUDENT B**

| AIRLINE AGENT | TRAVEL AGENT |
|---|---|
| Good afternoon **Singapore Airlines**. | Good afternoon. This is **Linda Lockhart** from Horizon Travel. |
| How may I help you? | Do you have a flight to **Ottawa** on **April 17**? |
| Yes, we have 2 flights on that date. Do you want the **5:40 a.m.** or the **17:25** flight? | I'd like to reserve a seat on the **17:25** flight. |
| Can I have the passenger's name, please? | The passenger's name is **Frank Johnson**. How much is the airfare? |
| It is **$1,510** plus taxes. | Can I have the reservation number, please? |
| Of course. The reservation number is **CZ 7TLV**. | Thank-you. |
| OR | |
| No, we don't fly to that city. | What airline flies there? |
| **Lufthansa** goes there. | Okay. Thank-you. |

**Part One:** You are an AIRLINE AGENT. Use the Flight Information below to answer the Travel Agent's questions. Fill in the chart below.

| Passenger's Name | Destination | Departure Date | Time | Airfare | RVSN. No. |
|---|---|---|---|---|---|
| | | | | | BHP5Z2 |
| | | | | | MM01W |
| | | | | | RM6CAQ |
| | | | | | M8V3S4 |

### FLIGHT INFORMATION

| Destination | Airline | Time | | Airfare |
|---|---|---|---|---|
| **Stockholm** | Singapore Airline (SQ)<br>Lufthansa Airline (LH) | 07:00<br>06:30 | 13:00<br>18:50 | $825.00<br>$875.00 |
| **Johannesburg** | Singapore Airline (SQ)<br>Lufthansa Airline (LH) | 08:40<br>14:15 | 22:20<br>19:45 | $1,350.00<br>$1,200.00 |
| **Beijing** | Singapore Airline (SQ)<br>Lufthansa Airline (LH) | 11:10<br>10:05 | 16:35<br>19:25 | $585.00<br>$665.00 |
| **Chicago** | Singapore Airline (SQ)<br>Lufthansa Airline (LH) | NO SERVICE<br>09:25 | <br>15:55 | <br>$1,020.00 |
| **Fiji** | Singapore Airline (SQ)<br>Lufthansa Airline (LH) | 12:30<br>06:50 | 21:10<br>18:40 | $1,800.00<br>$1,780.00 |
| **Ottawa** | Singapore Airline (SQ)<br>Lufthansa Airline (LH) | 05:40<br>NO SERVICE | 17:25<br> | $1,510.00<br> |
| **Prague** | Singapore Airline (SQ)<br>Lufthansa Airline (LH) | 16:15<br>00:40 | 23:30<br>14:15 | $1,130.00<br>$1,170.00 |

**Part Two:** You are a TRAVEL AGENT. Turn to the previous page.

## 7 READING

## Low Cost Airlines

1 A low-cost carrier (also known as a *no-frills* or *discount* carrier) is an airline that offers low fares but eliminates most traditional passenger services. Typical low-cost carrier practices include:

- a single passenger class
- a single type of airplane (reducing training and servicing costs)
- a simple fare scheme (typically fares increase as the plane fills up, which rewards early reservations.
- unreserved seating (encouraging passengers to board early and quickly)
- flying to cheaper, less crowded secondary airports (avoiding air traffic delays and taking advantage of lower landing fees)
- short flights and fast turnaround times (allowing maximum utilization of planes)
- simplified routes, emphasizing point-to-point transit instead of transfers at hubs.
- emphasis on direct sales of tickets, especially over the Internet (avoiding fees and commissions paid to travel agents)
- employees have multiple roles, for instance flight attendants also clean the aircraft or work as gate agents (limiting personnel costs)
- "Free" in-flight catering and other "complimentary" services are eliminated, and replaced by optional paid-for in-flight food and drink.

2 Low-cost carriers pose a serious threat to traditional "full service" airlines, since the high cost structure of full-service carriers prevents them from competing effectively on price-- the most important factor among most passengers when selecting a carrier.

3 Many major carriers launched their own no-frills airlines, such as KLM's Buzz, British Airways' Go Fly, Singapore Airline's Tiger, Delta's Song and United's Ted. However they have found it difficult to make a profit.

4 Today, some thirty years after the first flights, low cost airlines carry over 64 million passengers every year. They are a shining star in a bleak sky.

### COMPREHENSION

◆ **Answer the following questions.**

1. What are low cost airlines?
2. Name 7 low cost airlines?
3. How do passengers benefit from flying a low cost airline?
4. What are some differences between low cost airlines and full service airlines?
5. Do you think low cost airlines are successful? Why or why not?
6. Can you name 2 more low cost airlines?

## 8 ONE MORE TIME

☑ **Choose 9 vocabulary words from the table below. Fill out the ZINGO Card. Your teacher will call out the vocabulary word. When you hear the word on your ZINGO Card called out, raise your hand and answer the teacher's questions. The first student to answer correctly will receive a chip. Shout-out "ZINGO!" when you have 3 chips in a row.**

STRUCTURE:

**Teacher:** Do you have a "**business class**" word?
**Student:** Oh, I do!
**Teacher:** What vocabulary word do you have?
**Student:** I have a "**business class**" word.
**Teacher:** What is business class?
**Student:** It is a type of **airline class.**
**Teacher:** Yes, you're correct. Here's your chip.
**Teacher:** Thank-you.

| | | |
|---|---|---|
| Sky Team | One Way | Special Meal |
| First Class | Insurance Surcharge | Shoulder Season |
| Airport Tax | One World | Waitlist |
| High Season | Confirmed | Economy Class |
| Roundtrip | Business Class | Star Alliance |
| Wheelchair | Fuel Surcharge | Low Season |

ZINGO CARD

| | | |
|---|---|---|
| | | |
| | | |
| | | |

# Chapter 12

## *An Unforgettable Journey.*

## ❶ KEY VOCABULARY

| | | | |
|---|---|---|---|
| Itinerary | View | Sightseeing | Airtel |
| Package Tour | VIA | Excursion | Leisure |
| Brochure | Amenities | Promotion | Half/Full Day |
| Optional | Transfer | Explore | FIT |
| Attractions | Compulsory | Highlights | Gratuity |
| Charter Flight | Cancellation Fee | Adventure | Duration |

## ❷ WARM-UP

| Date | Departing From | Destination | Transportation | Departure | Arrival |
|---|---|---|---|---|---|
| August 2nd | New York, JFK | Lima, Peru | LP 531 | 23:30 | 06:10 + 1 |
| August 5th | Lima, Peru | Cuzco | LP 023 | 09:30 | 10:45 |
| August 8th | Cuzco | Machu Picchu | Tourist Train | 07:00 | 11:05 |
| August 9th | Machu Picchu | Cuzco | Tourist Train | 15:30 | 19:20 |
| | Cuzco | Lima | LP 095 | 20:55 | 22:15 |
| | Lima | JFK | LP 530 | 23:50 | 08:30 + 1 |

B
Flying Time (1hr 20mins) ______

C
Leaving (3:30) ______

D
Arriving (7:20PM) ______

E
LP 023 ______

A
START (JFK)

F
Overnight Stay ______

G
1st Destination ______

◆ **Write the name of the place under the picture using the itinerary.**

◆ **Put the pictures in the correct order.**

**1.** __A__ **2.** ______ **3.** ______ **4.** ______
**5.** ______ **6.** ______ **7.** ______

**STRUCTURE:**

**A:** Where am I going first?
**B:** You're going to **Tokyo**.
**A:** What picture is it?
**B:** It's picture **H**
**A:** How am I going to get there?
**B:** You're going **by boat**.

◆ **Practice with a partner.**

## ❸ LANGUAGE STRUCTURE

| TOURIST | TRAVEL AGENT |
|---|---|
| Which cities will I visit? | You'll visit Cape Town and Skakuza. |
| What attractions will I see in Cape Town? | You'll see Table Mountain and Robben Island. |
| Where will I stay? | You'll stay at the Capetonian Hotel. |
| How many nights will I stay there? | You'll stay there for 3 nights. |
| Where will I go next? | You'll go to Krugar National Park. |
| What will I do there? | You'll go on a safari. |
| How much is this package tour? | The total cost is $1,267 excluding taxes and gratuity. |

➤ **Work with a partner. Read the detail description of a tour to Peru. Use the Key Vocabulary Section on the previous page to fill in the blanks.**

### *A Tour of Peru*

**Day 2** ◆ **Lima**
Arrive in Lima early morning. __________ to your hotel for 2 nights. In the afternoon, go on a __________ city tour to __________ this beautiful city.

**Day 3** ◆ **Lima**
Day at ____________ in Lima.

**Day 4** ◆ **Cuzco**
Transfer to the airport for a short __________ flight. _____________ of the Sacred Valley in the morning. Return to hotel in the afternoon for ____________ activities.

**Day 5** ◆ **Cuzco**
______________ include a visit to a traditional market, Huayaccari Hacienda Museum, and a fortress town.

**Day 6** ◆ **Machu Picchu**
Transfer by train. During your 4 hours hike, you'll see ruins and enjoy a spectacular __________. Afternoon, relax in this magical place.

**Day 7** ◆ **JFK**
Rise early to see a stunning sunrise. Optional ____________ are available. Day at your leisure to ____________ the ruins. Night flight back to New York ________ Lima.

➤ **Work in groups of three.**
**A TOURIST is visiting your country for 4 days and 3 nights. Write a brief description of places you want him/her to visit.**

### *A Tour of* ____________________
**(country)**

**Day 1** ◆ ____________________ **(city)**
**Attractions:**
______________________________
______________________________
______________________________
**Hotel:**
______________________________

**Day 2** ◆ ____________________ **(city)**
**Attractions:**
______________________________
______________________________
______________________________
**Hotel:**
______________________________

**Day 3** ◆ ____________________ **(city)**
**Attractions:**
______________________________
______________________________
______________________________
**Hotel:**
______________________________

*Total Package Price:* $__________

## ❹ CONVERSATION

➢ **Practice the following dialogue with a partner.**

**Isabella:** Good afternoon. Peru Tours. How may I help you?
**Hansen:** I'm Hansen Gomez. I received **an itinerary** for the package tour to Peru. ❶
**Isabella:** Okay, I see that we've already **received your payment** for the tour. ①
What can I do for you Mr. Gomez?
**Hansen:** Yes, I'm wondering what optional **excursions** are available in Machu Picchu. ❷
**Isabella:** We offer **a hot-air balloon trip for $200** per person.
Would you like me to book it for you? ②
**Hansen:** Sure, that sounds **adventurous**. What time should I arrive at the airport on August 12th? ❸
**Isabella:** August 12th? But you're **scheduled** to leave on August 2nd. ③
**Hansen:** No, that's not correct. I want to leave on the 12th. Well, can you change the date?
**Isabella:** Let me see if I can change it now… oh, yes, but you'll have to pay **an extra $500**. ④
**Hansen:** $500? But I thought this was a **promotional offer**. ❹
**Isabella:** The offer is good until August 5th. Can I book you for the 5th?
**Hansen:** That's impossible. I can't make it. I'll just have to cancel the tour then.
**Isabella:** That's fine, Mr. Gomez, but there's 75% cancellation fee.
**Hansen:** I shouldn't have to pay anything! It was not my fault!

## SUBSTITUTION DRILL

➢ **Substitute with the words or phrases below:**

| Hansen | Travel Agent |
|---|---|
| ❶ a brochure<br>an e-mail<br>a fax | ① gotten your payment<br>debited your credit card<br>deposited your check |
| ❷ trips<br>tours<br>activities | ② bungee jumping for $ 125<br>mountain repelling(abseiling) for $145<br>paragliding for $190 |
| ❸ thrilling<br>exciting<br>awesome | ③ booked<br>supposed<br>confirmed |
| ❹ special offer<br>discounted package tour<br>cheap package tour | ④ an additional $500<br>a supplemental charge of $500<br>$500 more |

## 5 CHALLENGE YOURSELF

➤ **Work in a group of three. Use the information below and draw a line of the best route to take. Write down the mode of transportation and schedule in the space provided. Then write down 2 places you must see in each city.**

**Poland**

**Places to Visit:**

1) ____________________

2) ____________________

**London**

(start)

**Places to Visit:**

1) ____________________

2) ____________________

BA0852
19:00—22:20

**Czech Republic**

**Places to Visit:**

1) ____________________

2) ____________________

**Hungary**

**SCHEDULE**

| PLANE | TRAIN |
|---|---|
| Warsaw ➲ Budapest (MA 6843) ✈ 17:00 – 18:45 | Warsaw ➲ Budapest ✈ 13:13 – 23:47 |
| Warsaw ➲ Prague (OK 0783) ✈ 14:35 – 16:15 | Warsaw ➲ Prague ✈ 05:18 – 20:12 |
| Budapest ➲ Prague (OK 091) ✈ 14:15 – 15:20 | Budapest ➲ Prague ✈ 13:50 – 21:23 |
| Prague ➲ Budapest (OK 0790) ✈ 12:25 – 13:30 | Prague ➲ Budapest ✈ 07:30 –14:57 |
| Prague ➲ London (BA 0855) ✈ 12:40 – 13:45 | Budapest ➲ Prague ✈ 12:03 – 19:40 |
| Budapest ➲ London (BA 0867) ✈ 12:25 – 14:05 | Prague ➲ Budapest ✈ 12:35 – 19:47 |

| Warsaw – What to see? | Budapest – What to see? | Prague – What to see? |
|---|---|---|
| ◆ Old Town – 17th -18th century buildings/ Royal Palace<br>◆ Lazienki Park – Summer residence of last king<br>◆ Jewish Ghetto –Location of Spielberg's "Schindlers List" | ◆ Castle Hill – Royal Palaces, Churches, and Citadel<br>◆ Parliament House<br>◆ House of Terror – WWII Museum | ◆ Prague Castle – 9th century<br>◆ Charles Bridge – Built in 1357 with 30 statutes from the 18th century<br>◆ Jewish quarters – Various Monuments, museums, synagogues, and the old Jewish cemetery |

**STRUCTURE:** ➤ **Now prepare a group presentation of your itinerary.**

**A:** We depart **Bangkok** on **TG 698** at **17:05**. We arrive in **Phnom Penh** at **18:20**. Attractions in **Phnom Penh** include **exploring the Killing Field** and **the Royal Palace**.

**B:** After **Phnom Penh**, our next destination is **Ho Chi Minh City**. We take **VN 816** departing at **14:25**, and arriving at **15:15**. Some of the highlights are: **a visit to the Cu Chi Tunnel** and **excursion to Dalat**.

**C:** The final city on our itinerary is **Vientiane**. We arrive in **Vientiane** on **QV 525** at **10:55**. Sightseeing in this beautiful city includes **Wat Si Sakat** and **Pha That Luang**. Then we take the **10:30 TG 691** flight back to **Bangkok**. This is the end of our unforgettable journey. The total cost for this package tour is **$675**.

## ❻-1 PAIR WORK

**○ STUDENT A**

| TOURIST | TRAVEL CONSULTANT |
|---|---|
| Where am I going first? | You're going to **Madrid**. |
| How am I going to get there? | You're going by **plane**. |
| How long am I going to stay there? | You're going to stay there for **3** nights. |
| What attractions am I going to see? | You're going to see **the Prado & the Royal Palace**. |
| Where am I going to stay? | You're going to stay at the **Casa Blanca** Hotel. |
| Where am I going after that? | You're going to **Seville**. |
| How much does this package tour cost? | It costs $**1,979**. |

**Part One:** You are a TOURIST. Ask the Travel Consultant about your trip to Indonesia. Complete the chart with the missing information.

| CITY | TRANS-PORTATION | DURATION | ATTRACTIONS/ HIGHLIGHTS | HOTEL |
|---|---|---|---|---|
| | | | | |
| | | | | |
| | | | | |
| | | | | |
| | | | TOUR PRICE: | $ |

**Part Two:** You are a TRAVEL CONSULTANT. Answer the Tourist's questions.

| CITY | TRANS-PORTATION | DURATION | ATTRACTIONS/ HIGHLIGHTS | HOTEL |
|---|---|---|---|---|
| Amman | Plane | 2 days | Roman Theater / Dessert Castle | Le Meridian |
| Petra | Bus | 3 days | Tombs / Light & Sound Show | Crowne Plaza |
| Wadi Rum | Bus | 1 day | Lawrence Spring / Bedouin Dinner | Sunset Camp |
| Aquaba | Taxi | 2 days | Aquaba Castle / Ride a Glass Boat | Movenpick |
| | | | TOUR PRICE: | $1, 220 |

## 6-2 PAIR WORK

STUDENT B

| TOURIST | TRAVEL CONSULTANT |
|---|---|
| Where am I going first? | You're going to **Madrid**. |
| How am I going to get there? | You're going by **plane**. |
| How long am I going to stay there? | You're going to stay there for **3 nights**. |
| What attractions am I going to see? | You're going to see **the Prado & the Royal Palace**. |
| Where am I going to stay? | You're going to stay at the **Casa Blanca** Hotel. |
| Where am I going after that? | You're going to **Seville**. |
| How much does this package tour cost? | It costs $**1,979**. |

**Part One:** You are a TRAVEL CONSULTANT. Answer the Tourist's questions.

| CITY | TRANS-PORTATION | DURATION | ATTRACTIONS/ HIGHLIGHTS | HOTEL |
|---|---|---|---|---|
| Jakarta | Plane | 1 day | Botanical Garden / National Museum | Shangri-La |
| Yogyakarta | Plane | 1 day | Water Castle / Puppet Show | Radisson Plaza |
| Bali | Plane | 3 days | Tanah Lot Temple / Cultural Show | Bali Hyatt |
| Lombok | Ferry | 2 days | Gili Island / Monkey Forest | Alang Alang |
| | | | TOUR PRICE: | $ 950 |

**Part Two:** You are a TOURIST. Ask the Travel Consultant about your trip to Jordan. Complete the chart with the missing information.

| CITY | TRANS-PORTATION | DURATION | ATTRACTIONS/ HIGHLIGHTS | HOTEL |
|---|---|---|---|---|
| | | | | |
| | | | | |
| | | | | |
| | | | | |
| | | | TOUR PRICE: | $ |

## 7 READING

### A Crown Jewel In The Clouds

1 The legendary 'Lost City of Machu Picchu' is without a doubt the most important tourist attraction in Peru and one of the world's most impressive archaeological sites. Machu Picchu stands 2,430 m above sea-level, in the middle of a tropical mountain forest, in a beautiful setting.

2 In the 15th century a great Incan Emperor, built a holy city in the clouds on the mountain known as Machu Picchu (which means "manly peak"). This extraordinary city lies halfway up the Andes Plateau, deep in the Amazon jungle, high above the Urubamba River. The Incas had already abandoned Machu Picchu, due to a smallpox outbreak, when, in 1535, the Spanish defeated the Incan Empire. The city was then 'lost' for more than three centuries until the American explorer Hiram Bingham rediscovered it in 1911.

3 Machu Picchu has three areas; an agricultural, an urban and a religious area. The agricultural area consists of stepped terraces built on the slopes of surrounding mountains. The urban area is "U" shaped and has streets and stairwells that consist of a total of 3,000 steps, as well as water canals and courtyards. The most important religious areas are overlooking the Urumbamba Valley thousands of feet below.

4 At an elevation of 2,450 m (8,000 feet) Machu Picchu is only reached by train from Cuzco or on foot via the Inca Trail, a stone pathway paved by the Incas that passes through multiple other Inca creations. The hike finishes with a bird's eye view of Machu Picchu and gives the trekker a true taste of how the Incas saw their city.

5 The first sight of Machu Picchu is almost magical. The temples, fields, terraces, and baths appear to be part of the hillside itself...an imposing, elegant green paradise carved into its natural surroundings. This is truly a crown jewel in the clouds.

## COMPREHENSION

◆ **Match the words in Column A and Column B to make sentences.**

| ANSWERS | A | B |
|---|---|---|
| ________ | **1.** Machu Picchu means | **a.** by train or on foot. |
| ________ | **2.** Hiram Bingham | **b.** steps, canals and courtyards. |
| ________ | **3.** Machu Picchu was built by | **c.** "manly peak". |
| ________ | **4.** The Urban section has | **d.** an Inca Emperor. |
| ________ | **5.** You can reach Machu by | **e.** rediscovered Machu Picchu. |

## 8 ONE MORE TIME

☑ **Make groups of four. Each group rolls the dice. The group that rolls the highest is the Contestant (C). The teacher is the Host (H). The Host reads the questions. If the Contestant answers the question incorrect, the game is OVER! The Host will select the next Contestant.**

| No. | QUESTIONS | WINNINGS |
|---|---|---|
| 5 | **Q: This country, located in the Indian Ocean gained its independence in 1976.**<br>a) Seychelles b)The Maldives<br>c) Sri Lanka d) Madagascar | **$1,000,000** |
| 4 | **Q: Highlights in this country include Brasov, Fargaras Mts and Transylvania ...**<br>a) Bulgaria b) Romania<br>c) Croatia d) Hungary | **$500,000** |
| 3 | **Q: This was a former British Colony ...**<br>a) Macau b) Hong Kong<br>c) Bermuda d) Cayman Islands | **$250,000** |
| 2 | **Q: What is the biggest country in Asia?**<br>a) China b) India<br>c) Pakistan d) Russia | **$125,000** |
| 1 | **Q: Maccu Picchu is located in this country ...**<br>a) Paraguay b) Argentina<br>c) Bolivia d) Peru | **$64,000** |

**STRUCTURE:**

**H:** Do you want to be a MILLIONAIRE?
**C:** You betcha! We love to be the next Millionaire.
**H:** All right! Here's your chance. Good luck! (Reads the questions 1- 5) What's your answer?
**C:** This is a very hard question.
**H:** Well, you're in the "hot seat" now. You may use a lifeline if you wish.
**C:** That's a great idea! We'll **ask the audience**. The answer is **b**.
**H:** Is that your final answer?
**C:** You betcha!
**H:** You're **CORRECT**. You just won **$64,000**. Do you want to risk it on the next question?
**C:** **Yes,** we're going **for the Million Bucks!**

### LIFELINES

**REMEMBER: You can only USE each Lifeline ONCE. You may use all 3 Lifelines for any one question. Use them WISELY!**

*LIFELINE 1*

In this lifeline, you can ask the audience what they think the correct answer is.

*LIFELINE 2*

The next lifeline, you can phone a friend and ask him/her for the answer.

*LIFELINE 3*

When you use this lifeline, 2 wrong answers will be taken away, leaving 1 wrong and 1 correct answer.

# Chapter 13

## *The Boarding Gate Is Closed.*

## ❶ KEY VOCABULARY

| | | | |
|---|---|---|---|
| Boarding Pass | Scale | Seat Number | Visa |
| Gate Number | Weigh | Overweight | Departure Card |
| Hand Carry | Baggage Claim Tag | Departure Lounge | Flight Number |
| Window Seat | Checking-In | Excess Bags | Cancelled |
| Aisle Seat | Bulk Head Seat | Frequent Flier Number | Prior |
| Middle Seat | Boarding Time | Luggage Tag | Announcement |

## ❷ WARM-UP

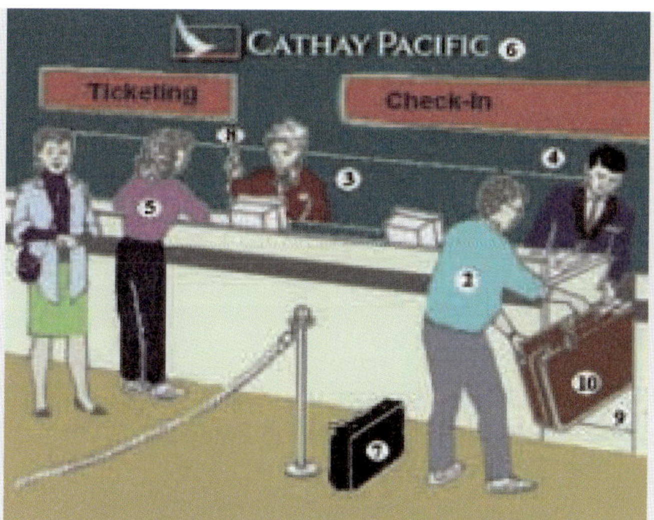


Hong Kong International Airport ❶

**Look at the picture on the left. Fill in the blanks below:**

**1.** The picture is at the ________________.
**2.** The passenger is ______________.
**3.** The woman behind the counter is a _______.
**4.** The man behind the counter is a ___________.
**5.** The woman is ___________ a ticket.
**6.** The passengers are flying __________ airline.
**7.** He has one piece of ______________.
**8.** There's only ___ seat available on this flight.
**9.** He's putting his luggage on the __________.
**10.** His bag is too heavy. It is _____________.

**Look at the picture on the right. Answer the questions below:**

**1.** What do you think this picture represents?
**2.** What is the passenger's surname?
**3.** What is the flight number?
**4.** Where is the passenger going?
**5.** What class is the passenger flying?
**6.** When is the passenger leaving?
**7.** Which gate is the passenger departing from?
**8.** Where is the passenger sitting?
**9.** What city is the passenger leaving from?
**10.** What's the passenger's frequent flier number?

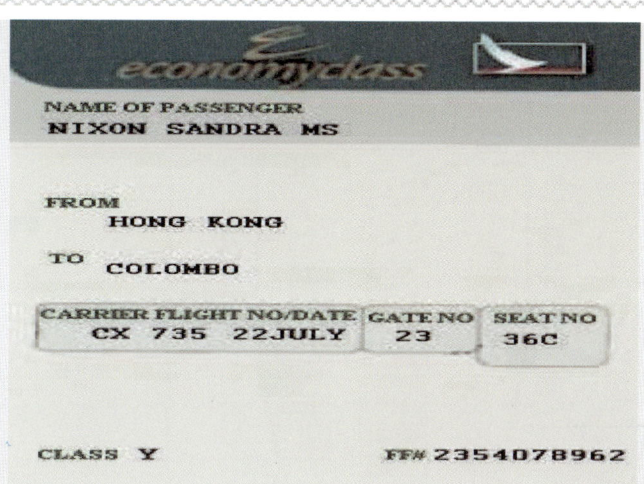

## ❸ LANGUAGE STRUCTURE

| CHECK-IN AGENT | PASSENGER |
|---|---|
| Good morning. Where are you traveling to? | I'm going to Rome. |
| May I have your ticket and passport, please? | Here you go. |
| Do you have any baggage to check-in? | Yes, I have two. |
| Could you place your bags on the scale? | Of course. |
| How many carry-on bags do you have? | Only one. |
| Do you have a seating preference? | Yes, I'd like an aisle seat, please. |
| Here's your boarding pass. Enjoy your trip! | Thank-you. |

➢ **Work with a partner. One student is a Passenger (P). The other is a Check-in Agent (A).**

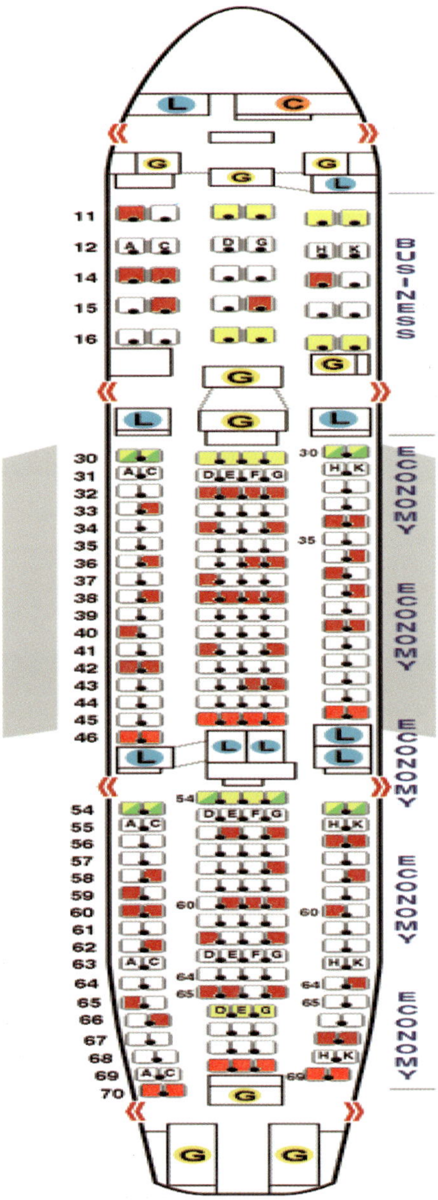


**STRUCTURE:**

**A:** How many bags do you have to check-in?
**P:** I have ______________ bag(s).
**A:** Please put your bag(s) on the scale.
**P:** All right.
**A:** Which seat do you prefer?
**P:** I'd like a/an __________ seat, please.
**A:** Here's your boarding pass. Your seat number is ______.
The gate number is ______. Your departure time is ______.
You should be at the gate 20 minutes prior to your departure time. Have a nice trip!
**P:** Thank-you.

◆ **You are a Check-in Agent. Look at the flight layout on the left. Use the chart below to check-in the Passenger. You must cross off (X) the assigned seats.**

◄ **NOTE: RED – Taken WHITE – Available**

| Passenger's Name | Seat No. | Check-In Luggage(s) (1, 2, etc.) | Gate No. | Departure Time |
|---|---|---|---|---|
| | ______ (Economy) | | 47A | 20:15 |
| | ______ (Business) | | 2B | 08:30 |
| | ______ (Economy) | | 18A | 16:45 |
| | ______ (Business) | | 21B | 00:50 |

◆ **Now switch roles.**

## ❹ CONVERSATION

➢ **Practice the following dialogue with a partner.**

**Check-In Agent:** Good morning. Where are you **traveling** to this morning? ①
**Passenger:** Good morning. I'm **traveling to London**. ❶
**Check-In Agent:** Could I see your ticket and passport, please?
**Passenger:** Sure. Here you are.
**Check-In Agent:** Please place your bags on the scale.
**Passenger:** Okay.
**Check-In Agent:** I'm sorry but your second bag **is overweight**. There will be a $150 surcharge for it. Do you want to pay for it? ②
**Passenger:** No, it's too expensive. I'll just **repack it** instead. ❷
…. 30 minutes later….
I'm ready now. **May I have** my boarding pass, please? ❸
**Check-In Agent:** I'm afraid **the boarding gate is closed**. ③
**Passenger:** What? But the flight doesn't leave until 10:30. I still have 20 minutes.
**Check-In Agent:** Yes, I know. But you will not have enough time to **clear customs**. ④
There is another flight tomorrow that leaves at 10:30.
**Passenger:** No! I **must be** there by tonight! I have an important meeting tomorrow. ❹
**Check-In Agent:** I'm afraid there is nothing I can do for you.
**Passenger:** There must be a way for me to leave today.

## SUBSTITUTION DRILL

➢ **Substitute with the words or phrases below:**

| Check-In Agent | Passenger |
|---|---|
| ① going<br>heading<br>off | ❶ going to Saigon<br>heading to Madrid<br>off to Istanbul |
| ② is too heavy<br>exceeds the weight limit<br>is over the maximum weight allowance | ❷ take something out<br>remove some stuff<br>transfer a few items to my first bag |
| ③ check-in counter is closed<br>you're too late<br>you just missed the final call | ❸ Can I get<br>May I receive<br>Could you issue me |
| ④ get to the gate<br>catch your flight<br>go through security | ❹ must arrive<br>need to get<br>have to be |

## 5 CHALLENGE YOURSELF

**Part One:** **Look at the two pictures below. There are 11 differences. Find and circle them.**

**Picture A**

**Picture B**

**Part Two:** **Complete the sentences using the words below. Then tick ☑ the correct box.**

| cloudy | departure gate | hand carry | sign | wheelchair |
|---|---|---|---|---|
| airplanes | earrings | ashtrays | carrying | under window |

| | Picture A | Picture B |
|---|---|---|
| **1.** The man is ______________ a bag. | ❑ | ❑ |
| **2.** The airport _______ says Dallas International. | ❑ | ❑ |
| **3.** The ______________ _______ is 69. | ❑ | ❑ |
| **4.** The woman in the _________________ is drinking coffee. | ❑ | ❑ |
| **5.** The _________ __________ bag is red. | ❑ | ❑ |
| **6.** There are two ____________. | ❑ | ❑ |
| **7.** There are two _______________. | ❑ | ❑ |
| **8.** The weather is rainy and _____________. | ❑ | ❑ |
| **9.** The briefcase is _________the chair. | ❑ | ❑ |
| **10.** One of the seats by the __________ is pink. | ❑ | ❑ |
| **11.** The woman is wearing _____________. | ❑ | ❑ |

**Part Three:** **Work in pairs. Student A reads the above sentences to Student B. Student B (with book closed) will say which picture the information is from. Take turns asking and answering the questions.**

## 6-1 PAIR WORK

**STUDENT A**

| PASSENGER | INFORMATION AGENT |
|---|---|
| **DEPARTURES** | **DEPARTURES** |
| What is **SQ 158**'s destination? | Flight **SQ 158** is going to **Jakarta**. |
| What time does it depart? | It leaves at **12:50**. |
| What gate does the flight depart from? | It leaves from gate **47A**. |
| What is the status of the flight? | The status of the flight is "**Now Boarding**". |
| **ARRIVALS** | **ARRIVALS** |
| What city is **SQ 158** arriving from? | Flight **SQ 158** is arriving from **Singapore**. |
| What time does it arrive? | It arrives at **13:25**. |
| What gate does the flight arrive at? | It arrives at gate **62B**. |
| What is the status of the flight? | The status of the flight is "**Landed**". |

➢ **Ask your partner for the information you need. Fill in the shaded areas below.**

**DEPARTURES**
**INTERNATIONAL FLIGHTS**

| City | Airline | Flight No. | Time | Gate No. | Status |
|---|---|---|---|---|---|
| | Emirates | EK 323 | | | |
| **Mexico City** | AeroMexico | AM 461 | 06:15 | 42B | Boarding |
| | Delta | DL 826 | | | |
| **Salzburg** | Austrian | OS 88 | 10:20 | 28B | Wait in Lounge |
| | Gulf Air | GF 5803 | | | |
| **Nassau** | Air Jamaica | JM 62 | 14:40 | 8A | Delayed / 22:35 |

**ARRIVALS**
**INTERNATIONAL FLIGHTS**

| City | Airline | Flight No. | Time | Gate No. | Status |
|---|---|---|---|---|---|
| | Avianca | AV 042 | | | |
| **Toronto** | Air Canada | AC 084 | 14:10 | 62B | Landed |
| | Alitalia | AZ 124 | | | |
| **Nairobi** | South African | SA 183 | 19:00 | 33B | Delayed / 01:00 + 1 |
| | Olympic | OA 079 | | | |
| **Shanghai** | Air China | CA 128 | 20:40 | 55B | Cancelled |

## ⑥-2 PAIR WORK

**STUDENT B**

| PASSENGER | INFORMATION AGENT |
|---|---|
| **DEPARTURES** | **DEPARTURES** |
| What is **SQ 158**'s destination? | Flight **SQ 158** is going to **Jakarta**. |
| What time does it depart? | It leaves at **12:50**. |
| What gate does the flight depart from? | It leaves from gate **47A**. |
| What is the status of the flight? | The status of the flight is **"Now Boarding"**. |
| **ARRIVALS** | **ARRIVALS** |
| What city is **SQ 158** arriving from? | Flight **SQ 158** is arriving from **Singapore**. |
| What time does it arrive? | It arrives at **13:25**. |
| What gate does the flight arrive at? | It arrives at gate **62B**. |
| What is the status of the flight? | The status of the flight is **"Landed"**. |

➤ **Ask your partner for the information you need. Fill in the shaded areas below.**

### DEPARTURES
### INTERNATIONAL FLIGHTS

| City | Airline | Flight No. | Time | Gate No. | Status |
|---|---|---|---|---|---|
| **Dubai** | Emirates | EK 323 | 00:30 | 36A | Departed |
| | Aeromexico | AM 461 | | | |
| **Boston** | Delta | DL 826 | 08:05 | 18A | Delayed / 12:45 |
| | Austrian | OS 88 | | | |
| **Amman** | Gulf Air | GF 5803 | 12:30 | 58B | Cancelled |
| | Air Jamaica | JM 62 | | | |

### ARRIVALS
### INTERNATIONAL FLIGHTS

| City | Airline | Flight No. | Time | Gate No. | Status |
|---|---|---|---|---|---|
| **Buenos Aires** | Avianca | AV 042 | 13:50 | 22A | Delayed / 21:10 |
| | Air Canada | AC 084 | | | |
| **Copenhagen** | Alitalia | AZ 124 | 15:35 | 17A | Landed |
| | South African | SA 183 | | | |
| **Athens** | Olympic | OA 079 | 19:25 | 46A | Delayed / 23:55 |
| | Air China | CA 128 | | | |

## 7 READING

### Running With the Bulls

1 Every year from July 7th-14th thousands pack into Pamplona to start Spain's most famous bull-running fiesta to honor Navarre capital's patron saint, San Fermin. Hundreds of locals and visitors risk their lives to outpace galloping, wild bulls as they run along an 800-metre stretch of the town's street.

2 After the daybreak of July 7th, runners (mainly young men) gather at the bottom of Santo Domingo, which is the starting line. They crowd together and sing a song that goes like this "We ask San Fermín, as our Patron, to guide us through the Bull Run and give us his blessing."

3 Then, as a rocket goes off, a number of fighting bulls are let out onto the streets. A second rocket is then let off to make sure everyone knows the bulls are loose in the street. The bulls run along the narrow street 825 meters (half a mile) to a bull ring. The runners dash along in front of the bulls, aiming to feel the breath of the bull on their backs, getting as close as possible - all whilst trying to avoid getting gored by their sharp horns. The way to do this is to start off slowly when the bulls are quite a distance behind. Then as they get nearer start running like mad! Runners look for a gap in the fence to slip through or jump over, or a space against the wall of the street. When the bulls finally reach the end of the street, they go into pens. They are killed later that day in a bullfight.

4 Originally only a few daring souls ran with the bulls but the adrenaline rush of running in front of a 750 kg bull has since caught on. People now journey from all around the world to run with the bulls.

### COMPREHENSION

◆ **One word in each sentence is incorrect. Cross out it out and write the correct answer.**

**1.** Pamplona is a city in Mexico.

**2.** The San Fermin Fiesta lasts for 9 days.

**3.** Runners gather at the starting line after sunset.

**4.** A gun goes off to signal the start of the run.

**5.** Runners try to outpace the cows.

**6.** At the end of the day, the animals are eaten.

**7.** Few people participate in the run.

## ❽ ONE MORE TIME

☑ **Make 3 groups. The teacher is the Host. The 3 groups are the Contestants.**

- **1 person from each group rolls a die. The dot(s) you get is how much money you'll start off with. (1 dot =$100, 2 dots=$200, etc.)**
- **A person from each group will do rock, paper, scissors. The winner chooses the category and rolls a die. To get a "Daily Double" you must roll a 6; and you may wage up to the maximum amount of money your group has. If you answer incorrectly, you loose that amount.**

| CHECK-IN | AIRLINE CODE | STATUS | AIRPORT |
|---|---|---|---|
| **$200**<br>You weigh your luggage on this. | **$200**<br>"LH" is a code for this airline. | **$200**<br>The flight is full. We'll put you on this. | **$200**<br>If you want to know the status of your flight, you should look on this board. |
| **$400**<br>Your bag is too heavy. | **$400**<br>"AF" is a code for this airline. | **$400**<br>The airplane has just arrived. | **$400**<br>You wait in this area for your departure. |
| **$600**<br>This is the number for your travel mileage. | **$600**<br>"CI" is a code for this airline. | **$600**<br>The airplane is late. | **$600**<br>This is the area for hand-carry inspection. |
| **$800**<br>7 types of information you would find on a boarding pass. | **$800**<br>"EK" is a code for this airline. | **$800**<br>Due to bad weather, UA884 is not departing today. | **$800**<br>This place is reserved for both first and business class passengers. |

**STRUCTURE:**

**Host:** Please choose a category.
**Contestant:** I'd like **Airline Code** for **$600**, please.
**Host:** (Reads)…**"VN" is a code for this airline**.
**Contestant:** What is **Vietnam Airline**?
**Host:** That's correct. You get **$600**.

**Daily Double**
**Host:** Please choose a category.
**Contestant: Airline code** for **$600**.
**Host:** How much are you going to risk?
**Contestant:** I'll risk **$1000**.
**Host:** (Reads)…**"VN" is a code for this airline**.
**Contestant:** What is **Vienna Air**?
**Host:** That's incorrect. You loose **$1,000**.

# Chapter 14

## *Come Fly With Me!*

## ❶ KEY VOCABULARY

| | | | |
|---|---|---|---|
| Turbulence | Foot Rest | Jetlag | Currency |
| Disembarkation | Blanket | Local Time | Refrain |
| Stowed | Remain Seated | Fasten | Lavatory |
| Headset | Life Jacket | Emergency Exit | Aircraft |
| Compartment | In-flight Magazine | Take-Off | Captain |
| Upright Position | Oxygen Mask | Duty Free Sales | Call Button |

## ❷ WARM-UP

**Part One:** **Label the gray areas using the above vocabulary.**

| | | | |
|---|---|---|---|
|  |  |  |  |
| A | B | C | D |
|  |  |  | 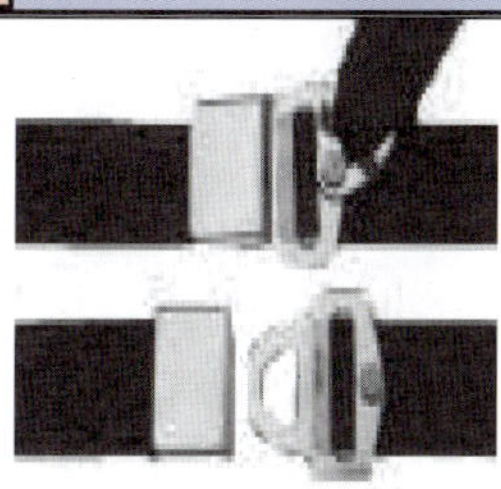 |
| E | F | G | H |
|  |  |  |  |
| I | J | K | L |

**Part Two:** **Fill in the chart. Label the above areas in ice-blue.**

**1.** You put your feet on this. ➲
**2.** This person flies a plane. ➲
**3.** This is found under the seat. ➲
**4.** You stow your carry-on in this. ➲
**5.** The seat must be in this position when the plane lands. ➲

| VOCABULARY | PICTURE |
|---|---|
| | |
| | |
| | |
| | |
| | |

## ❸ LANGUAGE STRUCTURE

| FLIGHT ATTENDANT | PASSENGER |
|---|---|
| Could you show me your boarding pass, please? | Certainly. |
| Do you need help with your bags? | Yes. I need to put this bag in the overhead bin. |
| Can I get you something to drink? | A can of Budweiser, please. |
| Which do you prefer, fish or chicken? | I'll have the fish. |
| Would you care for something to read? | The Wall Street Journal would be nice. |
| Do you want anything from the duty-free catalogue? | A bottle of Chivas Regal. |
| Would you like to change your seat? | Okay. I'll move to the window seat. |

➢ **Work with a partner. One student is a Flight Attendant (F). The other is a Passenger (P). Take turns being a Flight Attendant and a Passenger. Use the given structure below.**

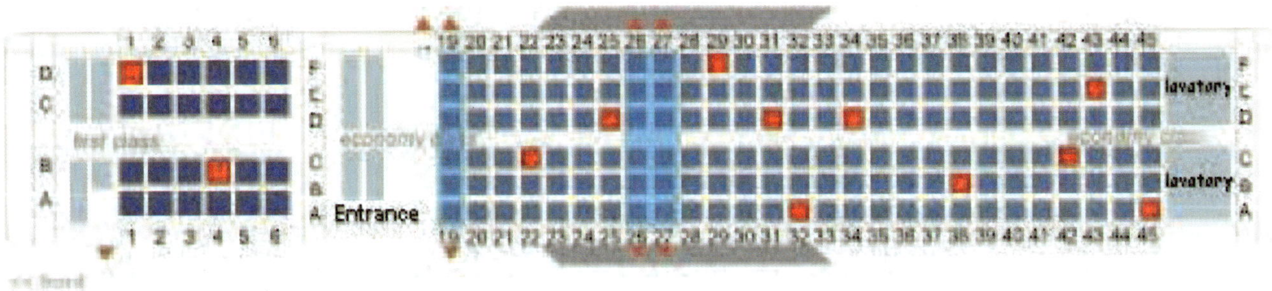


**STRUCTURE:**

**F:** Welcome aboard. May I see your boarding pass, please?
**P:** Here you are. I'm in **seat 38 B**.
Could you tell me where it is?
**F:** Sure. Go **back 20 rows**. It's the **middle seat** on your **right**.
**P:** Thank-you.
**F:** You're welcome. Have a pleasant flight!

**Passenger:**
Look at the seating arrangement.
Choose **4 seats (RED)** and circle them.
Ask the Flight Attendant where the seats are.

**Useful Vocabulary**

- ➢ Middle seat
- ➢ Window seat
- ➢ Aisle seat
- ➢ Go to the front
- ➢ Go back
- ➢ Right/Left

➢ **Use the vocabulary in the box. Fill in the blanks.**

**instruction upright landing seat pocket seatbelt signs**
**oxygen lavatories bound overhead take-off emergency**

**Flight Attendant's Announcement:**

Ladies and Gentlemen. Welcome aboard Asiana Flight 221 _______for San Francisco. Our flight time to San Francisco will be 10 hours after __________. Please fasten your _______ and bring your seat to an _________ position. Smoking is prohibited in both the cabin and the _____________. All carry-ons must be placed under your seat or in the __________compartment. Dinner will be served shortly after take-off. For your safety, there are 4 _______________ exits; 2 in the front and 2 in the rear. All exits are clearly marked with red ________. Your _____________ masks are in the overhead compartment and they will automatically drop when needed. In case of water ___________ life vests are under your seats. For more information about the safety features of this aircraft, please refer to the safety ________________card located in your _________________. Have a pleasant flight!

## ④ CONVERSATION

➢ **Practice the following dialogue with a partner.**

**Flight Attendant:** Welcome aboard.
**Passenger:** **Show me to my seat.** ❶
**Flight Attendant:** **Could I see** your boarding pass? Follow me, please. ①
**Passenger:** Sure. I'll follow you.
**Flight Attendant:** Here's your seat 38B. Please fasten your seatbelt. We're taking-off now.
.....Serving Meal....
We are serving **fish** and grilled chicken. Which do you prefer? ②
**Passenger:** I'll have the **grilled chicken and a double scotch**, please. ❷
**Flight Attendant:** Here you go. Enjoy your meal!
**Passenger:** This drink was really good. I **need another scotch** now. ❸
**Flight Attendant:** I'm afraid I can't serve you any more alcohol.
You've had **enough** to drink already. ③
**Passenger:** What do you mean I had **enough**? I only had two drinks. ❹
**Flight Attendant:** You had six drinks so far. Please sit down. You are **disturbing** other passengers.④
**Passenger:** No, I'm not. Why is it so difficult for you to get me another drink?
I believe I've paid my airfare just like everyone else here.
**Flight Attendant:** Just sit down and be quiet!
**Passenger:** No! I will not sit down until I get my drink!

## SUBSTITUTION DRILL

➢ **Substitute with the words or phrases below:**

| Passenger | Flight Attendant |
|---|---|
| ❶ Take me to my seat.<br>Bring me to my seat.<br>Where's my seat? | ① Can I look at<br>May I have<br>Please give me |
| ❷ steak and whisky on the rocks<br>shrimp and a glass of white wine<br>pork and a Bloody Mary | ② steak<br>shrimp<br>pork |
| ❸ want one more whisky on the rocks<br>would like another glass of white wine<br>will have one more Bloody Mary | ③ too much<br>plenty<br>a lot |
| ❹ too much<br>plenty<br>a lot | ④ bothering<br>annoying<br>upsetting |

## 5 CHALLENGE YOURSELF

➢ **Work with a partner. Complete the crossword puzzle.**

PUZZLE A

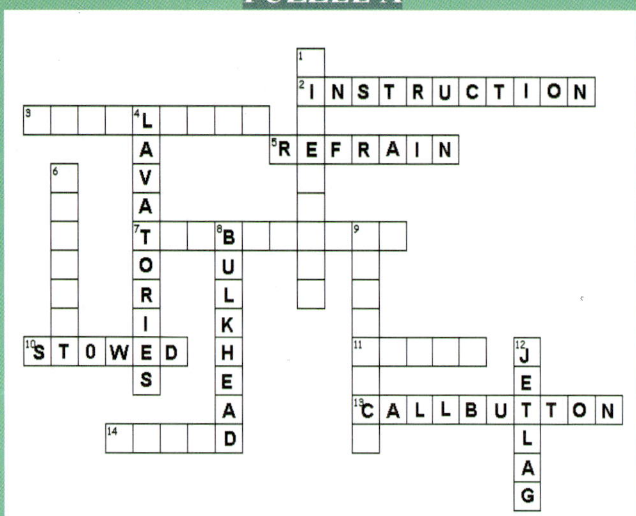

➢ **Look at the crossword puzzle.**
**Ask Student B for the clues.**

**STRUCTURE:**

**A:** What is number **15 across**?
**B:** Before take-off you do this with your seatbelt.
**A:** Is it "**buckle**"?
**B:** No, that's incorrect. The first letter is "**F**".
**A:** Is it "**fasten**"?
**B:** That's correct.

---

**ACROSS**

**2** This card gives you safety steps to follow.
**5** You are not permitted to smoke in the cabin.
**10** Hand-carries should be put away in the bin.
**13** If you need assistance you should press this.

**DOWN**

**4** "Bathrooms" are called these in an airplane.
**8** This seat has the most leg-room.
**12** You might have this after a long flight.

PUZZLE B

➢ **Look at the crossword puzzle.**
**Ask Student A for the clues.**

**STRUCTURE:**

**A:** What is number **15 across**?
**B:** Before take-off you do this with your seatbelt.
**A:** Is it "**buckle**"?
**B:** No, that's incorrect. The first letter is "**F**".
**A:** Is it "**fasten**"?
**B:** That's correct.

---

**ACROSS**

**1** It is when passengers get off the plane.
**3** The time of day in a particular area
**7** An air disturbance that causes the plane to shake.
**11** Emergency doors are called these.
**14** Another word for heading towards a destination.

**DOWN**

**6** When you feel cold you ask for this.
**9** A dollar is an example of this.

## 6-1 PAIR WORK

**STUDENT A**

| FLIGHT ATTENDANT | PASSENGER |
|---|---|
| Excuse me. Are you **Mr. Warner**? | Yes, I am. |
| Did you order a special meal? | Yes, I did. |
| What did you order? | I ordered a **vegetarian** meal **without broccoli**. |
| Would you care for something to drink? | Certainly, I'd like **sparkling water**, please. |
| Here you go. Enjoy your meal. | Thank-you. |

**Part One:** You role-play the following PASSENGERS.

- Choose a different meal and drink for each role.
- Write the number (1-12) and the letter (A-L) in the space provided.

### SPECIAL MEAL (Pre-ordered)

1. Seafood with shrimp
2. Seafood without shrimp
3. Vegetarian without broccoli
4. Vegetarian with broccoli
5. Diabetic - beef and vegetables
6. Diabetic - fish and rice
7. Fruit with strawberries
8. Fruit without strawberries
9. Low calorie chicken and rice
10. Low calorie beef curry and rice
11. Low cholesterol roast chicken and baked potato
12. Low cholesterol vegetables and tomato sauce

### The Most Popular Meal!

The Perfect Choice!

The Right Taste!

### DRINKS

A. Orange juice
B. Pineapple juice
C. Coke
D. Diet Coke
E. Red wine
F. White wine
G. Spring water
H. Sparkling water
I. Scotch on the rocks
J. Scotch straight-up
K. Coffee (Regular)
L. Coffee (Decaffeinated)

**FOR PASSENGER TO FILL IN**

| You are ... | Special Meal | Drink |
|---|---|---|
| Jessie White | ______ | ______ |
| Judy Peters | ______ | ______ |
| Amy Tan | ______ | ______ |

**Part Two:** You are a FLIGHT ATTENDENT. Turn to the next page.

## ⑥-2 PAIR WORK

**○ STUDENT B**

| FLIGHT ATTENDANT | PASSENGER |
|---|---|
| Excuse me. Are you **Mr. Warner**? | Yes, I am. |
| Did you order a special meal? | Yes, I did. |
| What did you order? | I ordered a **vegetarian** meal **without broccoli**. |
| Would you care for something to drink? | Certainly, I'd like **sparkling water**, please. |
| Here you go. Enjoy your meal. | Thank-you. |

**Part One:** You are a FLIGHT ATTENDANT.

- Ask what each Passenger had ordered.
- Write the number (1-12) and the letter (A-L) in the space provided.

### SPECIAL MEAL (Pre-ordered)

**1.** Seafood with shrimp
**2.** Seafood without shrimp
**3.** Vegetarian without broccoli
**4.** Vegetarian with broccoli
**5.** Diabetic - beef and vegetables
**6.** Diabetic - fish and rice
**7.** Fruit with strawberries
**8.** Fruit without strawberries
**9.** Low calorie chicken and rice
**10.** Low calorie beef curry and rice
**11.** Low cholesterol roast chicken and baked potato
**12.** Low cholesterol vegetables and tomato sauce

### The Most Popular Meal!

The Perfect Choice!

The Right Taste!

### DRINKS

**A.** Orange juice
**B.** Pineapple juice
**C.** Coke
**D.** Diet Coke
**E.** Red wine
**F.** White wine
**G.** Spring water
**H.** Sparkling water
**I.** Scotch on the rocks
**J.** Scotch straight-up
**K.** Coffee (Regular)
**L.** Coffee (Decaffeinated)

**FOR FLIGHT ATTENDANT TO FILL IN**

| Passenger | Seat No. | Special Meal | Drink |
|---|---|---|---|
| Jessie White | 33E | ______ | ______ |
| Judy Peters | 41C | ______ | ______ |
| Amy Tan | 20F | ______ | ______ |

**Part One:** You are a PASSENGER. Turn to the previous page.

## 7 READING

### An Ideal Seat for Economy Class

1 Chatting on a cell phone, surfing the Net from a laptop and watching video-on-demand will soon become the standard flying experience for economy class passengers. Within 2 years most airlines will have these features that will transform your airline seat into a personalized in-flight office.

2 Many passengers may cringe upon learning that the one safe haven from cell phone chatter will soon disappear. To offer some relief to passengers, the latest technology is designed to allow flight crews to block calls during sleeping periods on long flights or during take-off and landing.

3 Besides using cell phones, passengers will be able to use back-of-the seat screens to surf the Internet, select video and audio programs on demand, click on maps to see where the aircraft is and what points of interest are on the ground as well as under the water, shop duty free and even order your in-flight meals.

4 The most innovative idea is the ventilated seat. A moveable curved headrest supplies fresh outside air. There is a button on the armrest that can vary the temperature around their seat. According to the company, the system "decreases by a factor of 20 the chances of catching colds and other diseases on the aircraft".

5 So pack your bags and head off to your dream vacation. There is something special coming in the air. Flying economy class is becoming cheaper and more comfortable.

## COMPREHENSION

◆ **Circle the correct letter.**

**1.** The followings are features of back of the seat screen, except:
a) order your meal　　b) video on demand
c) able to surf the internet　　d) none of the above

**2.** Airline crew can block cell phone calls during
a) boarding　　b) movie time
c) sleeping time　　d) meal time

**3.** The ventilated seat has all of these features, except:
a) supplies fresh air　　b) decreases the chance of catching a disease
c) increases the chance of catching a cold　　d) can vary the temperature

**4.** This new technology will become available on most airlines in
a) 12 months　　b) 24 months
c) 4 years　　d) 3 years

# 8 ONE MORE TIME

☑ **Divide the class into 5 teams. The teacher is the Host. The 5 teams are the Contestants. Choose a name for your team. Write it on a piece of paper and hand it to the teacher.**

**INITIAL ROUND: The Host selects the first 4 Contestants.**

| Items | Descriptions |
| --- | --- |
| 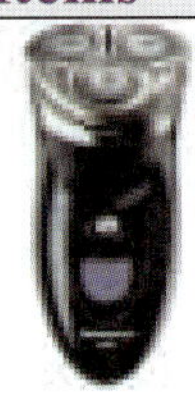 | **Philips Rechargeable Shaver**<br>* Quick charge in 3 minutes<br>* 100 minutes shaving time<br>* Comfort control<br>* Voltage selection<br>**PRICE:** $ ___ ___ ___ |
|  | **Chanel No.5**<br>* 50 ml EDT spray<br>**PRICE:** $ ___ ___ |

**STRUCTURE:**

**Host: Team A, B, C and D** come on down! You are the first 4 contestants on The Price is Right!
**Contestant:** We are the **A Team**. Glad to be on The Price is Right, **Bob**. We feel lucky today.
**Host:** (selects an item) The first item up for bid is a **Casio Watch**. (Reads the description) **Team A**, what do you think the actual duty free price is for this item?
**Contestant:** We think the duty free price is **$156**.
**Host:** The actual duty free price is **$200**. **Team A**, your bid was the closet to the actual price. Come over to the BONUS ROUND!

**BONUS ROUND: The winning team from the first round gets to play a PRICING GAME. They roll a die. The 1st (2nd, 3rd) number rolled corresponds to the 1st (2nd, 3rd) digit in the price of the item. If the number rolled is the 1st (2nd, 3rd) digit in the price, they will not loose a chip. On he other hand, if the number rolled is incorrect, the host will say whether the digit is higher or lower than the number rolled. Then the team will select a number. For each number the team is off, they must cross out (X) a heart. You must have at least one heart left to win this game.**

| STRUCTURE: | 1st Bonus Round | 2nd Bonus Round |
| --- | --- | --- |
| **Host:** Please roll a die.<br>**Contestant:** I got a **3**.<br>**Host:** I'm afraid **3** is not the **first** digit in the price of the item. The **first** digit is **higher** than a **3**.<br>**Contestant:** Is it a **4**?<br>**Host: No, it isn't**. The **first** digit is a **6**. **Please cross out 2 hearts.** | <br>**Digital Camera**<br>**Panasonic DMC-FZ20**<br>* 5 Meg pixel<br>* 12x Optical Zoom<br>**PRICE:** $ ___ ___ ___ | <br>**iRiver 40 GB MP3 Player**<br>* 1200 hours of music<br>* Large color display<br>* Voice recorder<br>**PRICE:** $ ___ ___ ___ |

**YOUR LIFELINE:**

# Chapter 15

## *I Have Nothing To Declare.*

## ❶ KEY VOCABULARY

| | | | |
|---|---|---|---|
| Carousel | Customs Form | Liquor | Claim your bags |
| Declare | Immigration | Perfume | Duty-Free Allowance |
| Landing Card | Purpose of Visit | Cartons | X-ray Machine |
| Prohibited Items | Terminal | Inspect | Citizen |
| Pleasure | Passport | Pay Duty | Resident |
| Period of Stay | Trolleys | Security Check | Commercial Merchandise |

## ❷ WARM-UP

◆ **Label each picture.**

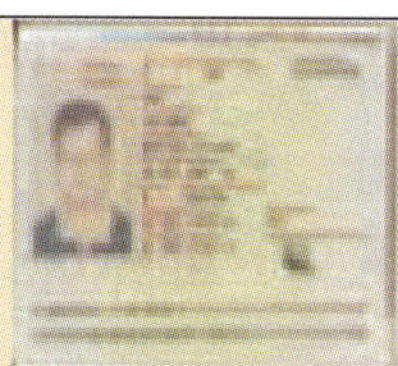
A

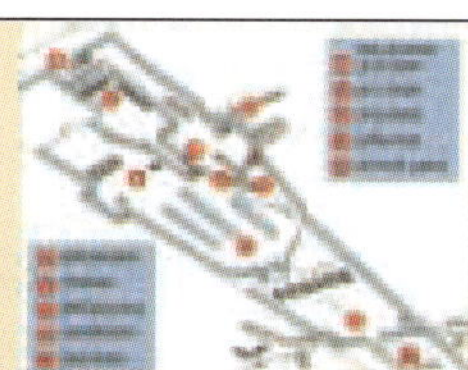
B

C

D

E

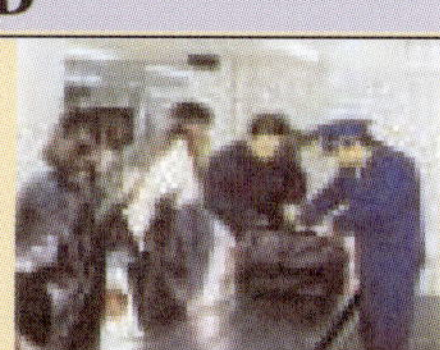
F

G

H

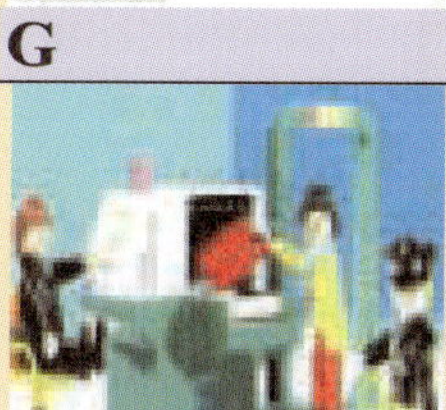
I

J

◆ **Match the pictures with the reasons below. The first one is already done for you.**

**Reasons Why I Think So …**

_A_ because it has a photo and personal information on it.
_____ because these carts are used to carry bags.
_____ because the immigration officer is checking the bags.
_____ because it's a drawing of an airport.
_____ because it has the word "Entry Card" on it.
_____ because these items are not permitted into the country.
_____ because this where passengers pick up their bags.
_____ because it shows how much you can bring into the country.
_____ because people are lining up to enter the country.
_____ because this machine photographs what's inside the bag.

◆ **Practice the structure below with a partner.**

**STRUCTURE:**

**A:** What do you think Picture **A** is?
**B:** I think it's **Passport**.
**A:** Why do you think so?
**B:** Because **it has a photo and personal information on it**.
And what do you think?
**A:** I also think that it's **Passport**.

# ❸ LANGUAGE STRUCTURE

| IMMIGRATION OFFICER | PASSENGER |
|---|---|
| Can I have your passport and arrival card, please? | Here you go. |
| Where are you coming from? | I'm coming from Italy. |
| What is the purpose of your visit? | Pleasure. |
| How long are you planning to stay here? | I'll be here for about a week. |
| Where will you be staying? | I'll be staying with my uncle in Dublin. |
| Have you been in Ireland before? | Yes, I've been here several times. |
| Do you have a visa? | Yes, I do. It's on the last page of my passport. |

➤ **Work with a partner. First, fill out your own arrival form. Then, ask your partner for the information you need to fill out his/her form.**

**For example:** **In what city was your visa issued?**
**It was issued in Rome.**

**FOR STUDENT A TO FILL IN**

U.S. Department of Justice
Immigration and Naturalization Service
OMB 1115-0077

Admission Number
Welcome to the United States
626443613 09

**I-94 Arrival / Departure Record - Instructions**

Type or print legibly with pen in ALL CAPITAL LETTERS. Use English. Do not write on the back of this form.

When all items are completed, present this form to the U.S. Immigration and Naturalization Service Inspector.

626443613 09

Immigration and
Naturalization Service
**I-94**
**Arrival Record**

1. Family Name
2. First (Given) Name
3. Birth Date (Day / Mo / Yr)
4. Country of Citizenship
5. Sex (Male or Female)
6. Passport Number
7. Airline and Flight Number
8. Country Where You Live
9. City Where You Boarded
10. City Where Visa Was Issued
11. Date Issued (Day / Mo / Yr)
12. Address While in the United States (Number and Street)
13. City and State

**FOR STUDENT B TO FILL IN**

U.S. Department of Justice
Immigration and Naturalization Service
OMB 1115-0077

Admission Number
Welcome to the United States
626443613 09

**I-94 Arrival / Departure Record - Instructions**

Type or print legibly with pen in ALL CAPITAL LETTERS. Use English. Do not write on the back of this form.

When all items are completed, present this form to the U.S. Immigration and Naturalization Service Inspector.

626443613 09

Immigration and
Naturalization Service
**I-94**
**Arrival Record**

1. Family Name
2. First (Given) Name
3. Birth Date (Day / Mo / Yr)
4. Country of Citizenship
5. Sex (Male or Female)
6. Passport Number
7. Airline and Flight Number
8. Country Where You Live
9. City Where You Boarded
10. City Where Visa Was Issued
11. Date Issued (Day / Mo / Yr)
12. Address While in the United States (Number and Street)
13. City and State

## ❹ CONVERSATION

➢ **Practice the following dialogue with a partner.**

**Customs:** Good afternoon. Can **I see** your passport, please? ①
**Passenger:** Sure, here it is.
**Customs:** Thank-you. Do you have anything to declare?
**Passenger:** Yes, I do.
**Customs:** What do you have?
**Passenger:** I have some **perfume**. ❶
**Customs:** How **much perfume** do you have? ②
**Passenger:** I only have **a bottle**. ❷
**Customs:** Do you have anything else?
**Passenger:** Yes, I have **two cartons of cigarettes**. ❸
**Customs:** What is the total amount of your gifts?
**Passenger:** It is **less than** $200. ❹
**Customs:** Could **you open** your bag, please? ③
**Passenger:** What?
**Customs:** And look at this! You didn't mention anything about these **diamond rings**. ④

"I have nothing to declare but my genius!"

## SUBSTITUTION DRILL

➢ **Substitute with the words or phrases below:**

| Customs Officer | Passenger |
|---|---|
| ① I have<br>you show me<br>I look at | ❶ liquor<br>watches<br>DVDs |
| ② much liquor<br>many watches<br>many DVDs | ❷ 2 bottles<br>3 watches<br>a couple |
| ③ I inspect<br>I see<br>I check | ❸ a pack of cigars<br>a video camera<br>a CD player |
| ④ gold necklaces<br>ruby bracelets<br>emerald earrings | ❹ about<br>approximately<br>around |

## 5 CHALLENGE YOURSELF

➤ **Work in a group of four. Listen to your teacher reads out the sentences. Write down the number (1-20) under the appropriate picture below.**

| Immigration Officer | Flight Attendant | Pilot | Travel Agent |
|---|---|---|---|
|  |  |  |  |
| ____ ____ | ____ ____ | ____ ____ | ____ ____ |
| ____ ____ ____ | ____ ____ ____ | ____ ____ ____ | ____ ____ ____ |

# *Who Says This?*

| QUOTES | |
|---|---|
| **1.** Ladies and gentlemen. Please fasten your seatbelt and make sure your seats are in the upright position. | **11.** If you're looking for a great place to stay in Marrakech, book a suite at Riad Kniza. It is very luxurious. |
| **2.** It will be high season in Fiji so I'd suggest that you book your flight as early as possible. | **12.** For dinner, we're serving chicken and beef. Which one do you prefer, chicken or beef? |
| **3.** There are 4 emergency exits on this aircraft; 2 are in front and 2 are in the rear. | **13.** The flight time to San Francisco is 10 hours and 20 minutes after take-off. |
| **4.** We're getting ready to descend to a lower altitude in preparation for landing. Please remain seated. | **14.** There are no seats available right now. But I could put you on a waitlist. |
| **5.** Excuse me, ma'am. Could you show me your passport and arrival card, please? | **15.** I'm afraid your visa has already expired. Please go to that visa section over there. |
| **6.** Here's your arrival card. Please fill it out before landing. If you need assistance, please ask anyone of us. | **16.** Ladies and gentlemen. Please open up your shade. In a few minutes we'll be passing over the Sahara Desert. |
| **7.** Please return to your seats and fasten your seatbelts. We're experiencing turbulence. | **17.** Your seat number is 38C. Go straight past the emergency exits. It's an aisle seat on your right. |
| **8.** What is the purpose of your visit to Vancouver? And how long will you be staying here? | **18.** I'm afraid you forgot to fill out the arrival card. Please go over there and fill it out. |
| **9.** We have a 4 nights and 3 days package to Cancun. Our promotional offer is $525, all-inclusive. | **19.** The weather in Zanzibar will be partly cloudy with the high of 35 degrees. |
| **10.** May I see your return ticket, please? Here are your passport and ticket. Enjoy your stay in Colombia. | **20.** I'd recommend that you purchase travel insurance before your trip to Hawaii. |

## 6-1 PAIR WORK

**STUDENT A**

| IMMIGRATION OFFICER | PASSENGER |
|---|---|
| Welcome to Alaska. May I see your passport, please? | Of course. Here it is. |
| Where are you coming from? | I'm coming from **Taiwan**. |
| What is the purpose of your visit? | I'm here **on vacation**. |
| How long are you planning to stay? | I'll be staying for **5 days**. |
| Where will you be staying? | I'll be staying at **the Hyatt Hotel**. |
| Have you been to Alaska before? | No, this is my first time. |
| Enjoy your stay in Alaska. | I will. Thank-you. |

**Part One:** You are an IMMIGRATION OFFICER. Ask the questions and fill out the form.

| Name | Nationality | Last Country Visited | Purpose of Visit | Intended Length of Stay | Local Address |
|---|---|---|---|---|---|
| Shawn Morris | Colombian | | | | |
| Charlotte York | British | | | | |

**Part Two:** You role-play the following PASSENGERS. Answer the questions.

| PASSPORT | PASSPORT |
|---|---|
|  **Susan Summers**<br>**Nationality:** New Zealander<br>**Expiration Date:** 2007/10<br>**Passport No:** 249773 |  **Jeff Pile**<br>**Nationality:** Canadian<br>**Expiration Date:** 2010/02<br>**Passport No:** VN357828 |

You're Susan Summers. Use this information.

**Coming From:** Auckland
**Purpose of Visit:** to study at a University
**Length of Stay:** 2 years
**Local Address:** the University Dormitory

You're Jeff Pile. Use this information.

**Coming From:** Thailand
**Purpose of Visit:** to see the sights
**Length of Stay:** 10 days
**Local Address:** a Hostel

## 6-2 PAIR WORK

**STUDENT B**

| IMMIGRATION OFFICER | PASSENGER |
|---|---|
| Welcome to Alaska. May I see your passport, please? | Of course. Here it is. |
| Where are you coming from? | I'm coming from **Taiwan**. |
| What is the purpose of your visit? | I'm here **on vacation**. |
| How long are you planning to stay? | I'll be staying for **5 days**. |
| Where will you be staying? | I'll be staying at **the Hyatt Hotel**. |
| Have you been to Alaska before? | No, this is my first time. |
| Enjoy your stay in Alaska. | I will. Thank-you. |

**Part One:** You role-play the following PASSENGERS. Answer the questions.

**PASSPORT**

**Shawn Morris**
**Nationality:** Colombian
**Expiration Date:** 2012/05
**Passport No:** 9162847

**PASSPORT**

**Charlotte York**
**Nationality:** British
**Expiration Date:** 2015/03
**Passport No:** ZT647251

You're Shawn Morris. Use this information.

**Coming From:** Colombia
**Purpose of Visit:** to visit my brother
**Length of Stay:** 3 weeks
**Local Address:** my brother's residence

You're Charlotte York. Use this information.

**Coming From:** London
**Purpose of Visit:** on business
**Length of Stay:** 5 Days
**Local Address:** the Hilton Hotel

**Part Two:** You are an IMMIGRATION OFFICER. Ask the questions and fill out the form.

| Name | Nationality | Last Country Visited | Purpose of Visit | Intended Length of Stay | Local Address |
|---|---|---|---|---|---|
| Susan Summers | New Zealander | | | | |
| Jeff Pile | Canadian | | | | |

## 7 READING

### The Terminal Man

1 He could be any passenger waiting for a flight, sitting patiently on a red plastic bench in Charles de Gaulle Airport's Terminal One,luggage piled neatly by his side. But Merhan Karimi Nasseri is going nowhere. He has been waiting for a flight out of France, he says, for over 10 years.

2 Nasseri was expelled from Iran over a decade ago for his political views. Banned from Iran, he went to Britain where he was refused political asylum. Merhan then bounced across Europe for several years and spent several months in prison for illegal immigration. In 1981, his request for political asylum from Iran was finally granted. Nasseri decided in 1986 on England with the hope of finding relatives there. He got as far as Paris, where in 1988 his briefcase containing his documents was stolen in a train station. Nasseri boarded a plane for London anyway. But when immigration officials at Heathrow Airport found he had no passport, they sent him back to Charles de Gaulle. At first, the French police arrested him for illegal entry. But as Nasseri had no documents, there was no country of origin to which he could be deported.

3 So he took up residence in the basement mall of Terminal One. Nasseri's red bench was his bed and living room. During Nasseri's first years in the airport, his basic needs were supplied by passers-by and airport workers. People bought him food, gave him money and listened with sympathy to his tale.

4 After fighting for years to leave the airport and apply for citizenship elsewhere, Nasseri was afraid to do so when the opportunity arose. Belgium offered Nasseri the chance to settle there, but he refused.

5 Nassari story was the inspiration of Steven Spieldberg's film "The Terminal" He received more than US$300,000 for the rights to his life story, but he hasn't touched most of it. He lives on a few euros each day, buying papers, food and coffee.

### COMPREHENSION

◆ **Write T if the sentence is true and F if the sentence is false. If it is false, make it true.**

**1.** Mr. Nasseri is from the Middle East. _____

**2.** Mr. Nasseri decided to emigrate to Paris. _____

**3.** His briefcase was stolen in a London train station. _____

**4.** Mr. Nasseri took up residence in the basement mall of Heathrow Airport. _____

**5.** He has lived at the airport for about 10 years. _____

**6.** Steven Spielberg's "The Terminal", was based on Mr. Nasseri's story. _____

**7.** The French police arrested Mr. Nasseri for illegal substances. _____

## 8 ONE MORE TIME

◆ **Divide the class into 2 Contestants. Roll the die. The winner gets to pick a category and describes the 8 words to his/her partner in 45 seconds. The team gets 1 point for each correct response. The winner gets to go to the Winner's Circle.**

### CATEGORY 1

**Things you find in a Duty-Free Shop**

| | |
|---|---|
| __ Cigarettes | __ Chocolate |
| __ Liquor | __ Shirt |
| __ Camera | __ Tie |
| __ Perfumes | __ Make up |

### CATEGORY 2

**Tourism Jobs**

__ Dealer

| | |
|---|---|
| __ Pilot | __ Cashier |
| __ Purser | __ Server |
| __ Chef | __ Bell Boy |

__ Immigration Officer

**STRUCTURE:**

**Host:** Please choose a category.
**Contestant:** I'll choose "Category 3 – **Honeymoon Destination**."
**Host:** You have 45 seconds to describe the words. Good luck. Go!

## Winner's Circle

◆ **Choose 2 people from your team. One will be the clue giver. The other is the receiver. The clue giver lists items that fit into the category. You must answer all 6 categories to win $25,000. All 6 categories can be randomly chosen.**

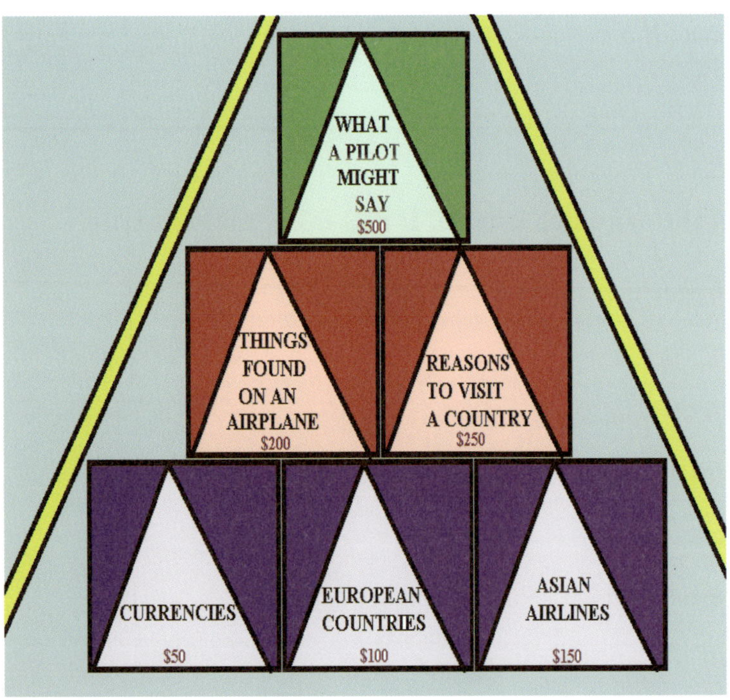

**STRUCTURE:**

**H:** Let's go to the Winner's Circle.
**G/R:** $25,000 sounds great. Let's do it!
**H:** Who wants to give the clues?
**G:** I'll give the clues.
**H:** You have 60 seconds to win the money. Select a triangle. Ready … Go!
**G: Korea, China, Japan.**
**R: Countries.**
**G: Singapore, Thailand, Indonesia.**
**R: Asian countries.**
**G:** Correct.
**H: Host G: Clue Giver R: Clue Receiver**

# Vocabulary review Chapter 1~15

## VOCABULARY REVIEW

◆ Write a sentence for each vocabulary word you've learned.

| Chapter 1 | Sentence |
|---|---|
| **1.** urgent | |
| **2.** unavailable | |
| **3.** asap | |
| **4.** appointment | |
| **5.** extension | |
| **6.** exclusive | |
| **7.** polite | |
| **8.** etiquette | |
| **9.** respect | |
| **10.** interrupt | |
| **11.** match | |
| **12.** disturb | |
| **13.** request | |
| **14.** switch | |
| **15.** upgrade | |
| **16.** inform | |
| **17.** patron | |
| **18.** forward | |
| **19.** occupied | |
| **20.** message | |

## VOCABULARY REVIEW

◆ **Write a sentence for each vocabulary word you've learned.**

| Chapter 2 | Sentence |
|---|---|
| **1.** nationality | |
| **2.** surname | |
| **3.** vacation | |
| **4.** prefer | |
| **5.** assists | |
| **6.** carry | |
| **7.** collect | |
| **8.** duties | |
| **9.** park | |
| **10.** manage | |
| **11.** capital | |
| **12.** famous | |
| **13.** occupation | |
| **14.** Language | |
| **15.** How many…? | |
| **16.** How long…? | |
| **17.** Which…? | |
| **18.** When…? | |
| **19.** Who…? | |
| **20.** How…? | |

## VOCABULARY REVIEW

◆ **Write a sentence for each vocabulary word you've learned.**

| Chapter 3 | Sentence |
|---|---|
| **1.** ETA | |
| **2.** ETD | |
| **3.** daily | |
| **4.** hourly | |
| **5.** every hour on the half hour | |
| **6.** delayed | |
| **7.** ahead of schedule | |
| **8.** depart | |
| **9.** arrive | |
| **10.** airfare | |
| **11.** cheap | |
| **12.** purchase | |
| **13.** every other day | |
| **14.** bound | |
| **15.** local time | |
| **16.** boarding | |
| **17.** cancelled | |
| **18.** half past | |
| **19.** bargain | |
| **20.** midnight | |

## VOCABULARY REVIEW

◆ **Write a sentence for each vocabulary word you've learned.**

| Chapter 4 | Sentence |
|---|---|
| **1.** handicapped | |
| **2.** facilities | |
| **3.** conference | |
| **4.** banquet | |
| **5.** costlier | |
| **6.** polluted | |
| **7.** thrilling | |
| **8.** famous | |
| **9.** quieter | |
| **10.** cheaper | |
| **11.** shuttle | |
| **12.** challenging | |
| **13.** safer | |
| **14.** luxurious | |
| **15.** comfortable | |
| **16.** laundry | |
| **17.** worse | |
| **18.** charming | |
| **19.** city center | |
| **20.** quicker | |

## VOCABULARY REVIEW

◆ **Write a sentence for each vocabulary word you've learned.**

| Chapter 5 | Sentence |
|---|---|
| **1.** rotary | |
| **2.** zebra crossing | |
| **3.** at the back of | |
| **4.** in the middle of | |
| **5.** around | |
| **6.** business center | |
| **7.** check-in | |
| **8.** ballroom | |
| **9.** ATM | |
| **10.** ladies' room | |
| **11.** opposite | |
| **12.** intersection | |
| **13.** overpass | |
| **14.** florist | |
| **15.** dry cleaners | |
| **16.** near | |
| **17.** north | |
| **18.** bridge | |
| **19.** between | |
| **20.** behind | |

## VOCABULARY REVIEW

◆ **Write a sentence for each vocabulary word you've learned.**

| Chapter 6 | Sentence |
|---|---|
| **1.** voucher | |
| **2.** confirm | |
| **3.** family name | |
| **4.** champagne | |
| **5.** contact | |
| **6.** vacancy | |
| **7.** mattress | |
| **8.** rate | |
| **9.** supplemental charge | |
| **10.** area code | |
| **11.** boutique hotel | |
| **12.** frequent | |
| **13.** baby crib | |
| **14.** special request | |
| **15.** service charge | |
| **16.** view | |
| **17.** trend | |
| **18.** payment | |
| **19.** reach | |
| **20.** booked solid | |

## VOCABULARY REVIEW

◆ **Write a sentence for each vocabulary word you've learned.**

| Chapter 7 | Sentence |
|---|---|
| **1.** key card | |
| **2.** request | |
| **3.** pamphlet | |
| **4.** complimentary | |
| **5.** signature | |
| **6.** escalator | |
| **7.** net | |
| **8.** overnight | |
| **9.** imprint | |
| **10.** next destination | |
| **11.** valid | |
| **12.** reception | |
| **13.** available | |
| **14.** wake-up call | |
| **15.** register | |
| **16.** full name | |
| **17.** zip code | |
| **18.** walk-in | |
| **19.** emergency contact | |
| **20.** fill in | |

## VOCABULARY REVIEW

◆ **Write a sentence for each vocabulary word you've learned.**

| Chapter 8 | Sentence |
|---|---|
| **1.** recommend | |
| **2.** fillet | |
| **3.** hidden | |
| **4.** pitcher | |
| **5.** refill | |
| **6.** special | |
| **7.** homemade | |
| **8.** sautéed | |
| **9.** grill | |
| **10.** A la Carte | |
| **11.** carafe | |
| **12.** dressing | |
| **13.** seafood | |
| **14.** condiment | |
| **15.** imported | |
| **16.** domestic | |
| **17.** vertical | |
| **18.** horizontal | |
| **19.** tip | |
| **20.** vegetarian | |

## VOCABULARY REVIEW

◆ **Write a sentence for each vocabulary word you've learned.**

| Chapter 9 | Sentence |
|---|---|
| **1.** local | |
| **2.** rejected | |
| **3.** located | |
| **4.** amount | |
| **5.** sent | |
| **6.** bought | |
| **7.** cost | |
| **8.** well-stocked | |
| **9.** check-out | |
| **10.** debit | |
| **11.** received | |
| **12.** enjoy | |
| **13.** bill | |
| **14.** transportation | |
| **15.** itemized | |
| **16.** feedback | |
| **17.** mistake | |
| **18.** international call | |
| **19.** room service | |
| **20.** apologize | |

## VOCABULARY REVIEW

◆ Write a sentence for each vocabulary word you've learned.

| Chapter 10 | Sentence |
|---|---|
| **1.** VIP | |
| **2.** roll | |
| **3.** bet | |
| **4.** spin | |
| **5.** minimum | |
| **6.** surveillance camera | |
| **7.** column | |
| **8.** row | |
| **9.** winning | |
| **10.** increase | |
| **11.** deal | |
| **12.** split | |
| **13.** wage | |
| **14.** same suit | |
| **15.** a pair of | |
| **16.** chips | |
| **17.** deck of cards | |
| **18.** even money | |
| **19.** pay-out | |
| **20.** dozen | |

## VOCABULARY REVIEW

◆ **Write a sentence for each vocabulary word you've learned.**

| Chapter 11 | Sentence |
|---|---|
| **1.** travel insurance | |
| **2.** code shared | |
| **3.** alliance | |
| **4.** connecting flight | |
| **5.** transfer | |
| **6.** airport tax | |
| **7.** reservation number | |
| **8.** issued | |
| **9.** allowance | |
| **10.** non-stop | |
| **11.** transit | |
| **12.** stopover | |
| **13.** booking class | |
| **14.** waitlist | |
| **15.** direct flight | |
| **16.** status | |
| **17.** currency | |
| **18.** benefit | |
| **19.** airline code | |
| **20.** surcharge | |

## VOCABULARY REVIEW

◆ Write a sentence for each vocabulary word you've learned.

| Chapter 12 | Sentence |
|---|---|
| **1.** highlights | |
| **2.** gratuity | |
| **3.** compulsory | |
| **4.** airtel | |
| **5.** FIT | |
| **6.** explore | |
| **7.** excursion | |
| **8.** amenities | |
| **9.** optional | |
| **10.** attractions | |
| **11.** cancellation fee | |
| **12.** package tour | |
| **13.** promotion | |
| **14.** route | |
| **15.** risk | |
| **16.** audience | |
| **17.** chance | |
| **18.** abandoned | |
| **19.** urban | |
| **20.** tropical | |

## VOCABULARY REVIEW

◆ Write a sentence for each vocabulary word you've learned.

| Chapter 13 | Sentence |
|---|---|
| **1.** bulk head | |
| **2.** prior | |
| **3.** baggage claim tag | |
| **4.** announcement | |
| **5.** excess bags | |
| **6.** boarding pass | |
| **7.** inspection | |
| **8.** overweight | |
| **9.** outpace | |
| **10.** gather | |
| **11.** departure gate | |
| **12.** information board | |
| **13.** repack | |
| **14.** aisle seat | |
| **15.** hand-carry | |
| **16.** briefcase | |
| **17.** landed | |
| **18.** economy class | |
| **19.** weigh | |
| **20.** counter | |

## VOCABULARY REVIEW

◆ **Write a sentence for each vocabulary word you've learned.**

| Chapter 14 | Sentence |
|---|---|
| **1.** special meal | |
| **2.** lavatory | |
| **3.** instruction | |
| **4.** pre-ordered | |
| **5.** low calories | |
| **6.** technology | |
| **7.** stowed | |
| **8.** headrest | |
| **9.** call button | |
| **10.** jetlag | |
| **11.** fasten | |
| **12.** emergency | |
| **13.** seat pocket | |
| **14.** refrain | |
| **15.** turbulence | |
| **16.** disembarkation | |
| **17.** features | |
| **18.** personalize | |
| **19.** transform | |
| **20.** ideal | |

## VOCABULARY REVIEW

◆ **Write a sentence for each vocabulary word you've learned.**

| Chapter 15 | Sentence |
|---|---|
| **1.** terminal | |
| **2.** declare | |
| **3.** pay duty | |
| **4.** cartons | |
| **5.** assistance | |
| **6.** crew | |
| **7.** random | |
| **8.** trolley | |
| **9.** Inspect | |
| **10.** duty free allowance | |
| **11.** illegal | |
| **12.** citizen | |
| **13.** resident | |
| **14.** immigration | |
| **15.** line up | |
| **16.** commercial value | |
| **17.** local address | |
| **18.** permit | |
| **19.** deported | |
| **20.** prohibited Items | |

# Answer Key
# Chapter 1~15

## Chapter 1

**Warm-Up**

**A.** 1) important-urgent 2) switch-change
3) right away /ASAP 4) asks-requests
5) taken-received

**B.** 1) Ms. Pines talked to Lucy Wong.
2) The message was for Mr. Jason Chang.
3) Ms. Pines works for Club Med.
4) Ms. Pines was Mr. Chang's fax number.
5) The two changes were the date and room type.

**Challenge Yourself**

**Part B**

1. Caller: Mr. Jason Chang
2. Company: Pacific Travel
3. Contact No: 416-225-2960
4. Reason for the call: Book a conference room
5. Why was the person unavailable:
   Mr. Johnson was on the other line.
6. Who answered the call: Anna

**Reading**

1. T 2. False (restaurant) 3. F (softy)
4. T 5. F (rude) 6. T

**One More Time**

(Bonus Round)
Sweden has 100.1% cell-phone penetration rate

## Chapter 2

**Warm-Up**

A) lifeguard B) porter C) concierge D) chauffeur
E) pilot F) purser G) cashier F) busboy

**Language Structure**

2) What 3) Where 4)When 5) Why 6) Which 7) Who

**Challenge Yourself**

**Part 1**

1) Vietnam: E,7,Q 2) Austria: I,4,X 3) Italy: G,12,V
4) Ireland: H,9,Z 5) Maldives: K,8,R 6) Israel: C,2,S
7) Mongolia: L,10,T 8) Kenya: F,11,P 9) Brazil: J,3,U
10) Turkey: A,5,W 11) Singapore: D,1,T/Z 12) India: B,6,Y

**Part 2**

1) hotel or resort/massages people
2) hotel/is a head waiter
3) hotel, restaurant, resort/opens doors
4) restaurant/prepares food
5) casino/hands out cards
6) airport/collects boarding passes
7) airline/flies an airplane
8) restaurant/helps servers
9) hotel/cleans rooms
10) restaurant/parks cars
11) resort/carries golf clubs
12) airline/in charge of cabin crew

**Reading**

1) females--males 2) models--nurses 3) 1970's--1960's 4) most--few 5) were-weren't 6) easy-- hard

## Chapter 3

**Warm-Up**

A) every hour on the half hour/every hour on the hour
B) once a week C) ETA/ahead of schedule
D) ETD/ delayed

**Reading**

1) Jetlag is the disturbance of your sleeping patterns after a long flight.
2) Some factors include change of sleeping patterns, lack of exercise, and stale cabin air.
3) Jetlag occurs because of the difference in time at your destination.
4) You should drink a lot of water, try and get some sleep, limit your alcohol intake and get up and stretch.
5) Traveling from west to east increase the chance of getting jetlag.
6) You should go to bed at the same time you normally go to sleep at home.

## Chapter 4

**Warm-up**

1) handicapped 2) fitness center 3) mini-bar
4) laundry 5) restaurant 6) Babysitting service

**Reading**

1) C 2) D 3) A 4) B 5) C

## Chapter 5

**Warm-Up**

1. I 2. E 3. B 4. A 5. F 6. C 7. H 8. D 9. G

**Language Structure**

1) straight/past/information center
2) corner/past/Sheraton Hotel
3) over/Ocean Street/between/dry cleaners
4) one/across/bus terminal

**Reading**

1) C 2) D 3) E 4) F 5) A 6) B

## Chapter 6

**Warm-Up**

1) Traveler's Check/$100
2) Mastercard/10-08/Peter Jones
3) Serviced Apartments
4) service charge and tax/room rate/Italy

**Reading**

1) a  2) b  3) c  4) c  5) d

## Chapter 7

**Warm-Up**

**Blue Box:** 1) address 2) Check-in 3) Check out 4) no. of nights/room type 5) no. of guests/room no. 6) method of payment/room rate(tariff)

**Pink Box:** 1) nationality 2) passport number 3) next destination

**Language Structure (Dialogue)**

Welcome to Manila Peninsula. How may I assist you?
You have a reservation for a double room for 1 night. Is that correct?
May I have your passport, please?
Please fill out this registration card.
How will you be paying Mr. Brown?
May I swipe your card, please?
Thank-you. You're in room 2010 which is on the 20th floor.
Yes, it does. Can I have a bellman bring the bags to your room?
It's served from 6:30-10:00 in the coffee shop. Enjoy your stay with us.

**Challenge Yourself**

**Part 1**

1)complimentary 2) nationality 3) view 4) key card 5) sign 6) overnight 7) hotel chains 8) register 9) bellboy 10) next destination 11) imprint 12) registration 13) pamphlet 14) facilities 15) front desk

**Part 2**

| N | G | I | S |  | C | B | E | L | L | B | O | Y | D | T |
|---|---|---|---|---|---|---|---|---|---|---|---|---|---|---|
|  | E |  |  |  | O |  |  |  |  |  |  | R |  | E |
|  | I | X |  |  | M |  |  |  |  |  | A |  | S | L |
|  | M |  | T |  | P |  | R |  |  | C |  | R | N | H |
|  | P |  |  | D | L |  |  | E | Y |  | E |  | I | P |
|  | R |  |  |  | I |  |  | E | T | G | R | V | A | M |
| O | I |  |  |  | M | S | K | M | I | S | I |  | H | A |
| V | N |  |  |  | E |  | T | S |  | E | I |  | C | P |
| E | T |  |  |  | N |  | T | I | W |  |  | G | L |  |
| R |  |  |  |  | T | R |  |  | N |  |  |  | E |  |
| N | Y | T | I | L | A | N | O | I | T | A | N |  | T | R |
| I |  |  |  | T | R |  |  |  |  |  | T |  | O |  |
| G |  |  | I |  | Y |  |  |  |  |  |  | I | H |  |
| H |  | O | F | A | C | I | L | I | T | I | E | S | O |  |
| T | N | K | S | E | D | T | N | O | R | F |  |  |  | N |

**Reading**

1) You can find the room of the future in the Hilton Hotel
2) The bathroom has a glassed in shower with computerized temperature control.
3) The bed has air pockets instead of a spring mattress and a remote control that can adjust the position of the bed.
4) This hotel room is located in California.

**One More Time**

1) walk in guest 2) complimentary 3) wake-up call 4) front desk 5) suite 6) conference room 7) registration form(card) 8) passport 9) chauffeur

## Chapter 8

**Warm-Up**

2) portfolio 3) date 4) description 5) reference no. 6) amount 7) balance 8) total due

**Language Structure**

1) check-in 2) check-out 3) made/was 4) sent/cost 5) had/Malinowa Restaurant/charge/38.25 6) Aug 2nd/had/Column Bar 7) dry cleaned on 8) charge was 9) was rented/cost 10) ordered room service 11) room charge/90 12) service charge 13) VAT 14) total

**Reading**

1) F-USA  2) F-1986  3) T  4) T  5) F-2
6) a scientific laboratory  7) T

**One More Time**

1) front desk 2) I would like a ----- room 3) Service charge and tax 4) registration form 5) overnight 6) twin room 7) Concierge 8) pool ,gym, restaurant, business center, conference room 9) housekeeping 10) bellboy 11) vacancy 12) complimentary 13) room service 14) chauffeur 15)check-out 16) explain 17) credit card, voucher, cash, travelers check 18) room rate/tariff 19) conference room 20) dry cleaned 21) You sent a fax and the charge is… 22) net 23)You had a drink at the pool bar and the charge is … 24) expired/denied

## Chapter 9

**Warm-Up**

Appetizers - Asparagus Soup/Shrimp Cocktail/ Caesars Salad
Entrée - Salmon/Venison/Fillet Mignon
Side Dish - Sautéed Eggplant/ Rice with Saffron/ Baked Potato
Drinks- Martini/Fresh Fruit Juice/Herbal Tea
Desserts- Sorbets/Apple strudel/Tiramisu

**Language Structure**
**Part One**
Taking Orders- take/I get/like to
Entrée- about your/want ,order/can I get
Appetizers- for, an/kind/about
Drinks- you, drink/something/Do, want
**Part Two**
Salad Dressing- Italian/French/Blue Cheese
Potatoes- Mashed/Roasted/French Fries
Cooking Method- Barbecued/Deep Fried/Poach
Eggs- Sunny Side Up/Omelette/Scrambled
Cooked Meat- Rare/Medium Rare/Well Done
Vegetables- Steamed/Boiled/Raw
**Reading**
1) Bali -- Maldives 2) French -- Divehi 3) 20 -- 14
4) Western---Maldivian 5) 2000 – 2005 6) elevator--stairs

## Chapter 10

**Warm-Up**
A) Roulette B) Baccarat C) Keno D) Slot Machine
E) Craps F) Poker G) Roulette H) Progressive Jackpot I) Craps J) Blackjack
**Language Structure**
A) Craps B) Blackjack C) Roulette
D) Caribbean Stud Poker
**Challenge Yourself**
1) Odd/Even- E 2) Street- H 3) First Five- J
4) Straight Up- A 5) Corner- I 6) Red/Black- D
7) Double Street- K 8) Column- B 9) Split- G
10) Dozen- C 12) All Numbers- F

**Reading**
1) d 2) f 3) a 4) c 5) b 6) e
**One More Time**
Puzzle 1 = I hit the Jackpot!
Puzzle 2 = What is the maximum bet?
Puzzle 3 = A pair is two of a kind.

## Chapter 11

**Warm-Up**
1) CDG is located in Paris, France 2) AF is Air France
3) OK means confirmed
**Challenge Yourself**
1) Freedom Travel 2) Mr. Jeffrey Michaels
3) roundtrip 4) 29 December 2004 5)No 6) No
7) 5110025074 8) Economy Class 9) Lufthansa Airline 10) Incheon 11) 24 February 2005 12) Casablanca
13) 20 kilos 14) Waitlist 15) CMN
16) No stopover allowed 17) W1,887,700
18) W162,000 19) Korean Won 20) Visa

**Reading**
1) Low cost airlines offer low fares without the perks.
2) Southwest Airlines, Air Arabia, Air Asia, Wizz Air,
Tiger Air, Ryan Air and Virgin Blue Airlines
3) Passengers save money when the fly low cost airlines.
4) Low cost airlines offer cheaper fares, don't provide free meals, have a single class and have unreserved seating.
**One More Time**
1) Season( high, low, shoulder)
2) Alliances (Sky Team, Star Alliance, OneWorld)
3) Class (First, Business, Economy)
4) Surcharge (Fuel, Insurance, Airport tax)
5) Status (confirmed, waitlist)
6) Type of Ticket (one-way, roundtrip)
7) Special Request (special meal, wheelchair)

## Chapter 12

**Warm-Up**
**Part One**
B) Cuzco to Lima C) Machu Picchu D) Cuzco
E) Peru to Cuzco F) Machu Picchu H) Lima
**Part Two**
2) G 3) E 4) F 5) C 6) D 7) B
**Language Structure**
Day 2: Transfer/half day/explore
Day 3: leisure
Day 4 charter/Sightseeing/optional
Day 5 Highlights
Day 6 view
Day 7 excursions/explore/via
**Reading**
1) C 2) E 3) D 4) B 5) A
**One More Time**
1) D 2) D 3) A 4) B 5) A

## Chapter 13

**Warm-Up**
**Hong Kong Int'l Airport**
1) airport 2) checking-in 3) ticket clerk
4) check-in agent 5) purchasing
6) Cathay pacific Airlines 7) hand carry
8) one 9) scale 10) overweight
**Boarding Pass**
1) boarding pass 2) Nixon 3) CX 735 4) Colombo
5) Economy Class 6) 22 July 7) Gate 23
8) Seat 36C 9) Hong Kong 10) 2354078962

**Challenge Yourself**

**Part One**

1) Dulles 2) Clouds 3) gate no. 4) one airplane 5) man carrying a bag 6) red bag is different 7) ashtray 8) woman in the wheelchair is drinking coffee 9) woman in the wheelchair is wearing earrings 10) bag is under the chair 11) chair next to the man in the blue suit is different

**Part Two**

1) carrying-A 2) sign-B 3) gate number-A
4) wheelchair-A 5) hand carry-B 6) airplanes-A
7) ashtrays-A 8) cloudy-A 9) under-A
10) window-A 11) earrings-A

**Reading**

1) Mexico--- Spain 2) 9---7 3) after—before
4) gun—rocket 5) cows—bulls 6) eaten—killed
7) hundreds—thousands

**One More Time**

**Check-In:**

$200-scale $400- overweight $600- frequent flier number $800- name, flight number. departure/arrival city, gate no, class, date, frequent flier number and airline name/logo

**Airline Code:**

$200 Lufthansa Airline $400 Air France $600 China Airlines $800 Emirates Airline

**Status:**

$200 waitlist $400 landed $600 delayed
$800 cancelled

**Airport:**

$200 information board $400 departure lounge $600 security area $800 VIP lounge

## Chapter 14

**Warm-Up**

**Part One:**

A) oxygen mask C) in-flight magazine
E) duty free sales F) emergency exit
H) seat belt K) compartment

**Part Two:**

1) foot rest-B 2) captain-D 3) life jacket-G
4) compartment-K 5) upright position-I

**Language Structure**

1) bound 2) take-off 3)seat belts
4) upright 5) lavatories 6) overhead
7) emergency 8) signs 9) oxygen
10) landing 11) instruction 12) seat pocket

**Challenge Yourself**

**Across**

2-instruction 3-local time
5-refrain 7-turbulance
10-stowed 11-exits
13-call button 14-bound

**Down**

1-disembark 4-lavatories 6-blanket
8-bulkhead 9-currency 12-jetlag

**Reading**

1) D 2) A 3) C 4) B

**One More Time**

Shaver-$110 Perfume-$80 Digital Camera-$526
MP3 Player-$415

## Chapter 15

**Warm-Up**

**Picture:**

A) passport control B) terminal C) duty free allowance D) immigration E) carousal F) inspect
G) landing card H) prohibited items
I) x-ray J) trolleys

**Matching:**

1) A 2) J 3) F 4) B 5) G
6) H 7) E 8) C 9) D 10) I

**Challenge Yourself**

Immigration Officer: 5,8,10,15,18
Flight Attendant: 1,3,6,12,17
Pilot 4,7,13,16,19
Travel Agent 2,9,11,14,20

**Reading**

1) T
2) F Paris---London
3) F London----Paris
4) F Heathrow---Charles De Gaulle
5) T
6) T
7) F substance----immigration